Holding Onto HOPE

10 Keys to Hold Onto Hope Even When it all Seems Hopeless

Kristy-Lea Tritz

Holding Onto Hope: 10 Keys to Hold Onto Hope Even When it all Seems Hopeless

Copyright 2016 © Kristy-Lea Tritz

Empower and Inspire Publishing

www.empowerandinspirepublising.com

contact@empowerandinspirepublishing.com

ISBN: — 13: 978-0-9936829-4-0

Published in: Canada, USA, UK, Australia

TABLE OF CONTENTS

Meet the Author   Pg. 5

Chapter 1: Hopelessness is Part of the Plan?   Pg. 7

Chapter 2: Holding Tight to Hope   Pg. 15

Chapter 3: Preparation: Embracing the Journey   Pg. 21

Chapter 4: Last Resort as First Resort   Pg. 27

Chapter 5: Personal Stories of Hope   Pg. 35

                        Nicolas Westgeest   Pg. 37

                        Debbie Franklin   Pg. 47

                        Autumn Stirling   Pg. 57

                        Janea Trapp   Pg. 67

                        Brenda Young   Pg. 77

                   Mofoluwaso Ilevbare   Pg. 93

                   Hristiana Geogieva   Pg. 105

Chapter 6: Looking forward with Renewed Hope: The 10   Pg. 113
Keys to Hold Onto Hope Even When it all Seems Hopeless

Kristy-Lea Tritz

Kristy-Lea Tritz is an International Best-Selling Author of 7 books.

She is a heart centred fertility support coach helping women who struggle with fertility and its related issues.

Through coaching, workshops, programs, retreats as well as facilitation of a supportive fertility group that meets weekly Kristy-Lea provides women with fertility challenges a safe place in which to learn, be encouraged and connect with others going through the same or similar journeys.

Kristy-Lea's journey to becoming a heart centered fertility support coach began out of her own ten year fertility struggles and journey. Her compassion for those she also saw struggling around her stirred within her a deep desire to let these women know they were not alone and provide them with all the information she had accumulated through her years of research and interviews with professionals in the field.

She now combines her vast knowledge from years of education in Early Childhood Education, Massage Therapy, Aesthetics, Aromatherapy, Art therapy, Personal Development, Coaching, Creative Writing, Speaking, Teaching and Training to help others.

Web: www.yourfertilitysupportcoach.com

Web: www.kristyleatritz.com

Facebook: www.facebook.com/yourfertilitysupportcoach

Twitter: twitter.com/kristyleatritz

LinkedIn: ca.linkedin.com/in/kristyleatritz

Instagram: https://www.instagram.com/kristyleatritz/

Pinterest: https://www.pinterest.com/kristyleat/

Chapter 1

HOPELESSNESS IS PART OF THE PLAN?

ARE YOU KIDDING ME!

Jeremiah 29:11

"For I know well the plans I have in mind for you, says the LORD, plans for your welfare, not for woe! Plans to give you a future full of hope."

Is this it?
Is this really all life has to offer?

She sat there on the edge of the bed contemplating yet another day of words thrown in her face, another day of cruelty in action, and another day of heartache. How could people be so cruel? Why couldn't they celebrate the fact that she wasn't like them, instead of crushing her for being different. As tears rolled down her cheeks she couldn't help but feel the world would somehow be better off if she wasn't in it.

Persecution and bullying was something I encountered nearly every day at school since I began attending. I remember clearly sitting in my grade two class knowing then that those around me chose their favourites and all others were forsaken, simply because they were different. It was something our teacher had instilled in us based on her actions. It was clear she had favourites. Those who gained her approval were counted among the "right list" and were treated dramatically different than those who were unlucky and made her "wrong list". I was one of those who somehow couldn't figure out how one could make it onto this "right list", making me an outcast.

Demonstrated clearly for the entire class to see was just how much she hated you. I felt deep compassion for other students who were also on the "wrong list". Some, when they would ask to go to the bathroom, were blatantly ignored and told to hold it. As you can expect, sometimes they just could not hold it that long and soon puddles formed beneath their seats, only encouraging the cruel behaviour from those on the "right list". I felt sorry for them.

Even as a young child, I wished I could somehow make things better. I wished I could stand up to my teacher. I wished somehow that I was stronger and that my voice would matter. I often found myself out in the hallway of that class for asking questions in math. You see math was never my strong area. I always felt it was important to understand something and if you didn't know how to do it you were to ask for help. However, due to the fact that I was on the "wrong list" my questions were not welcomed and so neither was I in the class. I was to sit in the hallway and do my math work by myself, it was hopeless!

Many times after this experience I encountered new ways in which, brick by brick, more hopelessness entered my life. It seemed that once the pattern began it created a snowball effect. That inability to share my voice and stand up for what I thought was right had followed me throughout the years. Fear began to cripple me. It took over my life and all the fight I thought I had left was silenced. It was as if my real self fell into a deep slumber. Walls were built to protect. I was crying inside. On the outside I wore a smile and exuded a joyful demeanour. It was part of the protection plan. If no one knew you were in a hopeless place then they couldn't add to it, they couldn't hurt you, right?

Have you been to that place of hopelessness? Ready to give it all up, seeing no point in continuing? Does one day seem to add to another passing by as if life is in fast forward and slow motion all at the same time? Have you found yourself asking the question, "Is this it?" Maybe you are there right now. Possibly that's why you picked up this book, because deep inside somewhere you know there has to be more.

Hopelessness can become a place in which it seems your life gets trapped. One lost ray of hope is replaced by even more shadows of darkness. Pretty soon there seems to be nothing shining in your life, no bright ray of hope, only darkness. It seems to overshadow you, follow you even when you try and break free from it. Repetitive patterns take place and you find yourself wondering why certain things keep happening. Asking yourself If there is any way out from underneath what's happening.

Maybe you have even found yourself waking up every day only to wish your eyes didn't open and when they do only wishing you could stay in the comfort and safety of the warmth the covers provide that surround you. Possibly you find yourself walking through the day like a zombie rather than a participant in your life or holding back tears all day. Sometimes even falling asleep at night becomes a struggle. You might find yourself eating more than you should or less

than you should because your emotions take over or it's something you feel you can control in your life.
Have you found yourself asking questions like:
Will it always be like this?
Will I ever find happiness?
Will this pain ever end?
Can my life get any worse?
Is hope or happiness even possible for me anymore?
Is God even listening to me?

Whether you experience an illness, bullying, rape, terminal diagnosis, broken relationships, trauma, or anything else, no matter where your hopelessness comes from remaining in a place of hopelessness can bring with it other life patterns.

Some of these patterns or effects can include:
• Eating Issues: Consuming to much food or to little food. Choosing unhealthy foods vs healthy foods. Controlling food as a means to feel like you have control over other things in your life. Eating based on emotions.
• Broken relationships with family, spouses, children: Shutting others out as a protective mechanism. Allowing anger to infiltrate. Ignoring the healthy needs of children and spouses. Withdrawing and spending too much time alone in isolation. Entertaining or even entering into intimate relationships outside of your marriage. Losing your temper or getting frustrated with your children over small, trivial things that really aren't important.
• Addictions: to things like food, alcohol, relationships, pornography, sex, really anything that is a deeply rooted repetitive pattern you can't seem to stop. Something that is unhealthy for you in one way or another. Something you seem to not be able to live without, like you are trapped. A

great way to tell if it might fall into this category is ask yourself: Do I feel guilty when I do this? Am I hiding it? Do I not want others to know I do this?

- Spiritual brokenness: Feeling like God isn't listening to you and you are losing relationship with Him. Feeling like you can't enter into prayer, or you can't pray at all. Feeling a distance between you and God that runs deeply.
- Recurring, repetitive patterns: Recognizing recurring or repetitive patterns in your life. Maybe things happen over and over and you are wonder why they keep happening, why situations in your life haven't changed no matter how hard you have worked at them, seeing patterns in relationships, experiences you have, and other patterns that you know need changing but are unsure why they keep happening and you don't really know how to change it.
- Deep loneliness and longing: This is a loneliness that seems to take over your life and drag you down, a longing that seems to take over your thoughts and feelings. It causes you to feel a deep yearning, like your life is not fulfilling.
- Suppressed creativity and utilization of your gifts / talents: You may find yourself stopping things you love doing, things that used to bring you joy, feeling blocked in these areas or a lack of desire to do them
- Disassociation: Feeling like you are someone else trapped in your body and ignoring your real needs, wants, desires etc. for the sake of living what others would consider a normal life, pretending to be happy and that everything is ok when it isn't just so you don't have to "be real"
- Unhealthy Compromising: Entering situations or relationships that are unhealthy and detrimental

- Broken personal boundaries: Compromising on what you would do or not do in your life. Allowing others to use you consciously or unconsciously. Inability to say "no" when you desire to or need to.
- Desperation that leads to negative consequences: An example of this could be if you are desperate to be with someone and not be alone any more, you may compromise on the type of person you would allow in your life, which could lead you into a deeper place of hopelessness and loss of personal power.

*These are included here not as a comprehensive list but as a starting point to help you become aware of other areas of your life where hopelessness may be connected to or maybe showing up as so as to provide you a place to start your journey back into a place of hope. It is only when you become truly aware of something that change can be created in that area.

Jeremiah 29:11 says, "For I know well the plans I have in mind for you, says the LORD, plans for your welfare, not for woe! Plans to give you a future full of hope."

You don't have to continue to drown in hopelessness. It took me journeying through my own hopeless places and spaces to come to the realization of how deeply hope is rooted. Even when you might think the only way out of hopelessness is giving up and giving in there is something more, you can have a new blueprint shown to you.

Hopelessness really is part of the plan at times. It can be part of the plan because it can draw you closer to a place of empathy for others, make you more understanding, lead you to beautiful adventure you may have been too afraid to take before, and even bring about a deeper relationship with God. When reflected on and journeyed through those places of hopelessness can be a great source of strength. When you're open to learning from it hopelessness can teach you many things and can even open new doors of possibility.

This scripture above is to remind you that there is a greater plan than the one you can see in front of you right now or the blueprint currently in your hands. God says to you in this scripture verse that He knows those plans WELL. It doesn't say He sort of knows them, but that he knows them WELL and that those plans really are ones for your welfare, for the good, not for the bad. Yes, times may come in your life where you don't understand that plan in that moment. This is completely normal.

It is through reflection that the beauty of those plans can be seen. It's important to remember that God turns everything good for those who love Him (Romans 8:28). This plan is not just a hopeful one but is FULL of Hope, not partially, not some, but FULL! May you know you are not alone as you journey through your own hopelessness to finding hope.

Exercise 1: Exploration of Hopelessness Roots Exercise

Let's begin to uncover some of the roots of hopelessness so that as you work your way through this book you will be able to start the healing process in the areas you identify.

1. I feel most hopeless about?

2. When I think back to the past these things still cause me pain?

3. I can identify with the patterns or effects listed above including:

4. When I am in a place of feeling hopeless I tend to?

5. I think for me what's stopping me from breaking free from this current place of hopelessness is?

Reflect on 1 Peter 5:7

Chapter 2

HOLDING TIGHT TO HOPE:

EVEN WHEN IT'S JUST A THREAD

Psalm 119:103
"How sweet to my palate are your promises, sweeter than honey to my mouth."

God is there beside you. He hasn't let you go. He has promised you that He will never abandon you.

Deuteronomy 31:6 says:

"Be brave and steadfast; have no fear or dread of them, for it is the LORD, your God, who marches with you; he will never fail you or forsake you."

God will always provide a solution to whatever struggle you are facing, He marches with you side by side, no matter how hopeless it seems. Psalm 119:103 reminds us that God promises are sweet to our palate and He keeps those promises. A reminder of this is the rainbow. God set the rainbow in the sky as a reminder of His promise when it came to Noah and the flood. You to shall have a rainbow in your life.

Those times when I raised my hand in math class and asked a question, to acquire the knowledge I was missing, without fail, I was sent out into the hallway to complete the work on my own.

The rainbow God sent to me in those moments of hopelessness was another teacher. More like an angel in disguise. Mrs. Laliberte was her name. She happened upon me by chance one day and asked me why I was outside in the hall. I proceeded to tell her that I had asked a question in math that I didn't understand. I also explained to her that it was because of what "list" I was on in class and that every math class this is where I found myself.

Her eyes were so kind, her presence so gentle. You see she had been sick with polo when she was young and carried with her some physical challenges because of it. This meant she had to use an electric wheel around chair or two arm canes to get around. I saw her as different and unique like myself. She was an inspiration to me.

Trust was easily established with her. Each time, without fail, she was there, every math class from that day on. Busy her class would be and she would step out into the hallway where she would find me sitting. She began helping me with any questions I had, always taking the time to listen and explain things to me. She didn't have to do this, I wasn't part of her class but for some reason she was there to help.

In this instance this was my God sent solution. Grade 2 class still had struggles and challenges, but they were made easier with the knowledge that Mrs. Laliberte was someone I could count on. There were times even during recess or lunch break that she would meet up with me during her supervision on the playground and we would walk and talk till the bell rang. She was my best friend. The Grade 2 teacher taught me segregation, separation, and favouritism, Mrs. Laliberte taught me acceptance of one's uniqueness, true compassion and giving beyond what was required.

Hopelessness is a real experience. In fact, it often includes a journey through the grieving process. If you have ever looked up "grieving process" online, you will see dozens of sites pop up explaining the stages of grief a person goes through during times of death for example. What I want to bring to your attention, is as you read the steps of the grief process think of the hopelessness you have felt or continue to feel.

Often you will see a great similarity between the processes of grief and places you have journeyed through while experiencing hopelessness. It is my belief that as you go through trauma or other instances that create hopelessness in your life you are indeed going through a journey of grief as well.

You are mourning the loss of what happiness once was as it is replaced by hopelessness. You become overtaken by it, possibly consumed in thoughts over it. The heart and soul hold onto that experience and can be deeply wounded by whatever circumstances surrounded you in that place where you began to experience that hopelessness.

As this process begins to happen over and over it becomes like that grimy buildup around your bathtub if you don't clean it. Pretty soon it is a noticeable ring and if you don't do something about it fairly quickly it will be very difficult to remove. The same is true for the grief journey that accompanies hopelessness. What once held happiness and hope now holds onto pain and hopelessness.

In order to remove or in this case work through what really is the cause one must be willing to "clean" out the ring of grim left behind. Hopelessness is part of that grim. It is an after affect. It doesn't just pop up one day in your life and take root. There is always something that lies within which was the cause. Outside factors have had an effect, but they can only hold you hostage in that place of hopelessness if you let it.

Taking this one step deeper, one could say, that hopelessness is the barrier to hope. In fact, if you take a closer look at the word hope"less"ness you will see that it includes the word "less". You don't see the word "none" at all do you? It isn't hope"none"ness, it is hope"less"ness, "less" so in truth it isn't that you don't have hope, you just have less than you did before. (This can be due to the effect of the trauma, situation, circumstance or whatever caused the place of hopelessness in your life to sprout.)

If you know that then you know it is possible to become filled with hope again. Take a glass of water for example. If it has less than you want to drink in the glass what would you do? You would go and fill it, right? So then the real question is how do you become hope"full" again? How do you step from this place of hope"less"ness into hope"full"ness? What is it that can fill that cup back up? In all honesty this step of the process may be the most difficult because it asks you to do an internal reflection. To go to that place of pain, right to the root, uncover it, examine it, and really work through it.

Sometimes it means that you may need to reach out to others in your life. It can also mean speaking with a councillor or life coach who can help you work through the pains as they come up. You are not called to travel this journey alone. Don't be afraid to let others who are trustworthy help you as you find your way through the it all.

Your string of hope might be see through right now. Maybe you can even see some threads beginning to break. Possibly you can barely keep a grip on it. However, that string of hope, no matter how small is your lifeline.

God is that lifeline and He is the only way to adding more hope into your life and becoming hope"full". No human can fill that void within you. No substance can fill it. Nothing but the grace and love of God can fill those voids. Whatever you do don't let go. No matter how hard it is to see that tiny thread of hope, keep a firm grasp on it.

While it is still a glimmer in your life hold onto the knowledge that there will never be a time, no matter how difficult, that you will become hope"none"ness. It doesn't exist! Just like Jesus came to the earth as a human to bring us the hope of eternal life so too He will be there walking beside you, often carrying you. If you are in a place right now where you feel that even a glimmer of hope can't be found, I encourage you to continue to hold on. Just as hopelessness is a journey there is also a journey back to a hope filled life.

Exercise 2: Reflect to Heal

1. Take some time to journal and reflect on what may be causing your hopelessness on a deeper level.

2. Find someone you can trust and who will be not only a great support to you but also listener and go over what you have uncovered with them.

3. Write down ways in which God has brought "rainbows" into your life.

Reflect on Matthew 11:28-29

Chapter 3

PREPARATION: EMBRACING THE JOURNEY

Romans 15: 13
"May the God of hope fill you with all joy and peace in believing,
so that you may abound in hope by the power of the Holy Spirit."

Did you know that there are certain seeds that need a forest fire in order to germinate and grow? Does this make the seed hopeless that life will never come? Of course not! In due time it will blossom. In fact it was meant to blossom out of something seen as a bad thing. Just like an acorn doesn't need something outside of it to become a tree. Everything it needs to become that tree is contained within it. Now all it needs is the right circumstances to grow into that tree. In this case it needs the forest fire, it needs the process that fire takes the forest through, it needs the nourishment that the forest fire will bring to it. Without the forest fire it cannot have life.

Right now you may not feel that you have everything you need to overcome what hopeless lies within your life, but you really do have all you need. God has planted it within you from birth. The right circumstances just need to rise. Hope never goes away it's there within. How would you know what hope was if you didn't experience those periods of hopelessness. How would you know you are missing out on something good if you never experienced the bad? How would you know that there is something better? You wouldn't.

It is the times often looked at as bad or unpleasant that actually teach you what it means to have the opposite. If you didn't know what it was like to win at something you would think that losing is all there is. Often times it is said you truly begin to appreciate something when it is gone. This is actually a good thing. It allows you to know that life doesn't have to stay the way it is. That change is possible and those changes can bring about even greater things in your life. Sure just as the fire hurts other things in the forest so to the things you experience can bring hurt. Out of its ashes though you will experience that new life!

What's happening in your life here and now really is a preparation. If you're willing to take what's going on and ask yourself what is the lesson I am to learn from what's going on? What is it that God wants me to see and know from this? How can my life become better from what I am experiencing? How can I take this fire that I'm experiencing right now and use it as fuel for future growth?

Right now what you're going through may make you feel badly inside but those feelings are only one part of the equation. Those feelings are really there to let you know it's time to pay attention. There is something requiring you to be really and truly present in that moment. There is also the importance of taking action. What will you do with the lessons you're learning? How can you help others with what you've learned from what you've overcome and are currently overcoming? It's important to take every opportunity to listen to that internal voice. You know the one that God has placed within you. The one that acts as your warning device. It is there to help teach you and guide you.

Be really present in those moments and really open to what is happening for you, in you and around you.

When you're able to look beyond, what you feel and are experiencing right now, you will begin to see that even though it's difficult you will make it through. Hope will begin to return. Why? It is because there is a purpose even in pain. It comes down to whether you are willing to allow that pain to be used for a purpose or whether you will allow it to eat away at you. God wants to fill you with hope, joy and peace. Are you open to receiving it?

Embracing the difficulties in life's journey can bring about some of the most trying times for you, but it can also bring about some of the most amazing experiences you will ever have. I encourage you to draw closer in these moments to the Holy Spirit allow His peace to flow within you. Also, in the evening, remember to read the word of God in the Bible. Immerse yourself in the words that he has for you, those words of peace, perseverance and His faithfulness.

By embracing this part of your journey you are also embracing the preparation. You may not know, at this point in time what God has called you to do and sometimes it may seem unclear that there even is a call for you. I want you to know that there's a call for YOU. A very special call. A call that is unique to you. You were called to great things. Out of your pain and out of your experiences will come part of that call. You may be able to use your own life story to help others who are in a place in their lives where they also feel like giving up. You can be, at this point, a light to shine into their lives. You'll be the one who will bring hope to their lives.

If you don't know what it's like to go through something it is much more difficult to help others around you who are going through their own pain. It's more difficult, as well, to be able to identify with others who are in suffering. It's important to take suffering as a great gift. Suffering is not something to be feared, it is something to be embraced, because it is what teaches us. It teaches compassion, patience, forgiveness and the importance of living life to the fullest. Hopelessness can be a part of this suffering that you may experience in your life as part of that growth and teaching process. The tests are so that you might have the ability to testify to the greatness that can come from them.

Exercise 3: Using your experiences

1. How open are you to learning from the experiences you are going through right now as preparation for what may come in the future?

2. What are some experiences that you have gone through that may help others who are going through similar experiences right now?

3. What are some great lessons you have learned along the way?

4. If you currently are experiencing the fire right now what are some steps that you can take to use that fire as a learning experience?

Reflect on Hebrews 4:16

KRISTY-LEA TRITZ

Chapter 4

LAST RESORT AS FIRST RESORT

John 15:5
"I am the vine, you are the branches. He who abides in me and I in him, he it is that bears much fruit, for apart from me you can do nothing."

If you were given an Aloe Vera plant to take care of would you know what to do with it? Most of you reading this would know either how to take care of it so it would grow strong healing leaves or if you didn't know how to take care of this type of plant you might know who to ask or where to look up the needed information to care for the plant.

John 15:5 begins by telling us that God is our vine and we are the branches. If a vine is cut from its roots, would the branches remain and only the vine fall? If I took an Aloe Vera plant and chopped it off at the roots leaving only the top portion would it still sprout its healing leaves? No, in fact it is the vine that ultimately decides whether there will even be branches. I haven't seen any trees, that when cut from its base and the roots destroyed, leaves behind the branches it once held. If this was to happen the branches would die. It would be the furthest reach of these branches that would begin to die off first. So to it is if you are not connected to your vine, Christ. Your hope begins to first fade, then die off slowly at first but as more of it dies off this death of hope is accelerated.

God loves you so much that He is willing to be your support as you begin a process of renewing your hope. He is willing to be the centre from which you will sprout and be fed the nourishment you need. Looking at an Aloe Vera plant as an example, if you were to take a piece of its healing leaf what happens? What ends up happening is the end of the piece you took from will heal over. It continues to have life. Yes, sometimes during life there will be pain, scars, hurt, difficulties and struggles, but God is there always sustaining you as the vine. For it is from him where your nourishment will come. He will hold you up when you find it too hard to continue on. That's why it is important to turn to Him as a first resort instead of a last resort.

Jesus is like the sun in your life. He showed his love ultimately by dying on the cross so that you might have an example of hope. If you were to take the Aloe Vera plant and hide it in the dark where no sun shone on it what would happen? Most likely within a few days or even weeks it would die. Allow Jesus to shine into those places of your life you find most difficult, for it is in the isolation of darkness where death of hope occurs. However, if you were to place the plant in sunlight it would thrive.

Acts:13:47 says:

"For so the Lord has commanded us, 'I have placed you as a light for the gentiles, that you may bring salvation to the end of the earth."

This passage explains the importance of surrounding yourself with others who can be a light to your life. When you are going through the toughest of times and losing hope

it is of utmost importance that you surround yourself with
that light.

1 John 1:7 says:

*"But if we walk in the Light as He Himself is in the Light, we have
fellowship with one another, and the blood of Jesus His Son
cleanses us from all sin."*

Again this passage is revealing to you how important being
in that light is. This is an important part of continued hope,
because when things that have been in the dark are brought
to the light, you can forgive, find forgiveness, heal, and be
renewed.

Just as water is needed for a plant to grow, also you must
allow the Holy Spirit to water your life with the gifts He has
for you. These gifts will not only help you deepen your
spiritual life and allow you to enter deeper into that vine/
branch relationship with God, but it will also provide you a
place of renewed hope. God has blessed you with the gifts
you have been given because it is in those gifts where you
will feel most alive. Take for example someone who loves
painting. When they are painting they feel happy, whole,
hopeful, they feel alive! Take time to explore those gifts you
have been given because it is in them where you may find
your hope growing.

1 Corinthians 6:19-20 says:

*"Do you not know that your body is a temple of the Holy Spirit
who is in you, whom you have from God, and that you are not*

your own? For you have been bought with a price: therefore glorify God in your body."

The Holy Spirit dwells within you. Your body is a temple. If we take the Aloe Vera plant as a visual example with the pot representing your body. The pot can hold the water necessary to sustain the plant. Everything you place in the pot will affect the plant. If you fed the plant milk would it grow and have life? What if you fed it Pepsi or juice? Or tried to give it a cookie? Would that work. No, why? Because if you feed the wrong thing to the plant it will die! So to God calls you to feed your body those things in which will feed your spiritual growth life.

Prayer is one way in which you feed your body in this way. Without prayer over a long period of time you will surely begin to feel a death from within you. It is at this time where most experience that deep loneliness, that sense of loss, the diminishing of hope. Without this food your relationship with God will suffer, with your spouse or children and even with others around you. Your hope will continue to fade and you might even find yourself isolating. It would be like that branch that was without its vine. It cannot be sustained, it cannot continue to grow. God wants to be your vine He wants to sustain you!

Romans 12:2 says:

"Do not be conformed to this world, but be transformed by the renewing of your mind, so that you may prove what the will of God is, that which is good and acceptable and perfect."

Renewing your mind is an important step in renewing your hope filled life as well. Your mind can be like a broken record playing thoughts, images, injustices, angry words, really anything plays over and over and over, tearing you down. Renewing your mind allows God to become the forefront again. It allows more space for the good and great things.

Renewing your mind can be difficult at first, you may have to be consciously doing it at first. The more you do it the more it will "just happen" because the more transformed you will become. It is like the plant. A plant doesn't have to think about growing, it just does! Anything you allow into your mind it all has an influence and effect on you.

John 10;10 says:

"The thief comes only to steal and kill and destroy; I came that they may have life, and have it abundantly."

He came so that you may have life and have it ABUNDANTLY. He didn't say well...I think I will only reserve abundant life for people with blue eyes, or big feet, or brown hair. No, He came so that you could have life in abundance.

Jeremiah 29:12-14 says:

"When you call me, when you go to pray to me, I will listen to you. When you look for me, you will find me. Yes, when you seek me with all your heart, you will find me with you, says the LORD, and I will change your lot;"

Seek Him with ALL your heart and He will truly change your lot.

Exercise 4: Be Renewed

1. What are some things that bring you joy in your life?

2. How can you begin to incorporate more of these gifts that bring you joy?

3. In what ways do you feel you could renew your mind and life? Is there anything that is toxic in your life or that holds you in that place of hopelessness?

4. Who can you reach out to in your life that might be a light for you?

Reflect on Hebrews 13:6

KRISTY-LEA TRITZ

Chapter 5

PERSONAL STORIES OF HOPE

Within this chapter you will find stories from several individuals who wanted to share their stories of hope with you. These stories were written just for you. They were written from the hearts As you read these stories you will find renewal of your own hope.

Thank you to the following for sharing their personal stories:

Nicolas Westgeest

Debbie Franklin

Autumne Stirling

Janea Trapp

Brenda Young

Mofoluwaso Ilevbare

Hristiana Georgieva

KRISTY-LEA TRITZ

Nicolas Westgeest

Nicolas Westgeest is a meat cutter and has practiced his craft since the age of 12 in his father's butcher shop. He enjoys spending time with his family and helping others deepen their faith.

Facebook: www.facebook.com/opendoorprayergroup

LIFE IS WORTH LIVING!

It's hard to know where it all began, somewhere between the time I was born up until the time I turned 33. During the early years of my life depression and anxiety were the norm. I didn't recognize it in my own life as much as in the life of my father and one of my brothers. As early as the first grade, fear and anxiety had a firm grip on my life. Feelings of being inferior to others and fear of trying new things was a common theme. I wasn't afraid to try new things, really it was I was afraid of failure. Frozen in the fear, time sometimes seemed to stand still. Someone could be talking to me yet I would hardly comprehended a word. Concentrating was difficult.

Throughout adulthood this followed me around like a ball and chain. I found this to be especially true after the birth of our daughters. I wasn't sure that I was a reliable or good father. Yet at the same time it seemed that my career was on track. I was able to supply for the physical needs of our family. it was the Spiritual or emotional needs I felt I lacked in providing. I felt my wife and daughters deserved so much more than, at the time, I felt capable to provide. It was slowly catching up to me. When I turned 33 the wheels fell off. There was no more getting away from it. One day at work I just stopped functioning. Everything seemed to close in on me. Weekly visits to the psychiatrist were not helping and I was sinking deeper into depression. Suicidal thoughts were a constant companion. I even thought that my family would be better off without me. From somewhere inside I began to cry out to God. Pleading with Him to please help me! I cried out saying that if He was real and really care for me to please help me, please.

God was real! He did hear me. He sent an older brother of mine to me. My brother had heard of a retreat centre that he believed held the answer to many of my problems. After discussing it with my wife, we decided what the heck, there was nothing to lose and who knows maybe, just maybe, everything to gain. So I went. Little did we realize but our lives were about to change drastically.

It was September 18, 1991 when I drove up to Hinton AB. The Way of Holiness Prayer Retreat House, was a place of solitude and peace. It was surrounded by mountains. Upon entering I was greeted by Sister Mary Joe Cassidy. She showed me my room and invited me to a prayer meeting that was to be held that evening. Having nothing to lose I thanked her and said that I would attend. Little did I know that my life would be changed forever that evening. My life was changed in so many ways. The greatest being that God showed me He loved me and that my life was worth living. God pulled me out of the depths of despair that night and set my life on a course of thanksgiving. For my family the journey has not been without bumps and bruises, life has a way of throwing those curve balls at you, it is however the way you deal with them that matters. It is the assurance that God your Father loves you deeply and cares what happens to you. It is the free offering of your own hardships, back to the Father, through His Son Jesus, that gives meaning even in the roughest waters in your life.

When you are able to rely on God and you learn through life's difficult moments, it is through these moments that you experience God covering you. Each time you experience Him pulling you through these times it becomes easier. It's just like sharing a problem with a friend. Sometimes you can't find the solution on your own, but with their help a solution can be found together. You can tell others to rely on God, but until you experience Him covering you in life's difficult moments it's just words.

God is my best friend. I can tell Him anything knowing that he won't give me a strange look or say things like, "why are you being so dumb." He does however encourage you to pick up your cross and follow Him. Your crosses will then not be heavy any longer. This is not to say that the crosses you carry don't exist only that they cannot defeat you.

This really became apparent to me on a beautiful spring

morning. May 15, 2015 began like any other working day. 3:30 am my alarm went off. I got up, washed and spent time in prayer before getting into my car. I began the half hour drive to work. Recently, I had been making an effort to stop before work at the church in a nearby town. My time spent in the small Church seemed to prepare me for the work day.

As I left the church and got back onto the highway. It was a dry road in front of me, the weather was clear, it was still dark out but my headlights lit the road in front of me. I was talking to Jesus. Telling him I loved Him, that all I had was His, and for Him to do with me whatever His will. As I rounded the corner I noticed in the distance headlights coming from my left, towards the stop sign that stopped the traffic not traveling on the highway. I was alarmed when the headlights began to move across the highway! There was no way I was going to be able to avoid colliding with him. There just wasn't enough room for me to maneuver out of the way as I slammed on my brakes and tried to steer in an avoidance direction as best as possible. In the blink of an eye it all happened! I said, "Jesus I think I'm going to meet you face to face today?" I repeated this statement one more time. Then immediately told Him, "I don't think I'm ready!"

It was as though time had slowed. My thoughts and the sensations that followed seemed to take longer than the few seconds. My senses were heightened to a level that they had never been nor have been since that day. I was able to take everything in. I had the sense of someone with me in my car. An interior voice instructing me to brake and turn the wheel to the right. Doctors later told me this was probably what ended up saving my life.

The dust rose in the air upon impact and a strange smell filled my nostrils as the airbag deployed. My body slammed against the airbag. I was then flown back into my seat. I could see out my windshield as my vehicle travelled into and out of a ditch, through a farmers fence and into his field, before finally coming to a stop, where often on my way to work I would see his horses grazing. Smoke was rising from the engine as the water and coolant from the rad leaked out. My first reaction, after my vehicle came to a stop, was to thank Jesus because I knew that I was alive! I had survived the impact! This was apparent to me because of the intense pain I now felt in my chest. I repeated over and over, thank you Jesus, thank you Jesus.

Pushing the door open as far as I could, I unbuckled the seat belt and rolled out out onto the ground, out of instinct, not really thinking through that I might be injured. I tried to get up, at that point becoming aware there was something wrong with my leg. I couldn't put weight on it. Looking into the car I noticed my coffee mug on the floor board with the lid still closed. I said, "Oh thank you Jesus, you even saved my coffee !" Pulling myself back into the vehicle I took out my coffee mug, leaned against the driver's side of my car and took a swallow of coffee. It was so good to be alive! I thought quite differently from the days when I didn't want to live before. Now I was so grateful, pain and all, to be blessed to still be alive.

Within minutes the driver of the other vehicle was standing in front of me asking if I was okay. He asked me to sit down and asked me if he could check on my ankle, ribs and neck, apparently his father at one time was a paramedic and he had some first aid training. Nothing seemed broken or so he thought. Little did either of us know the extant of my injuries. As he was finishing the driver that witnessed the accident stopped. He had already called 911 and told us the fire department, ambulance and police had been notified and dispatched. I had been travelling at 100 kilometres per hour and thought it was amazing that both the driver of the other vehicle and myself were alert and alive.

The smoke was clearing by the time the fire department arrived and only a few minutes later the ambulance was pulling up. One of the EMT's came over and along with one of the firefighters helped me through the ditch onto the road and to the side of the ambulance. Once there I was instructed by the EMT to enter the ambulance where they could better assess my condition and decide which hospital to take me to. while in the ambulance and on the gurney it became clear that my injuries were worse than I had first thought. The EMT's allowed me to phone my wife on my cell phone and let her know what had happened. It was on the third try that she awoke, since no one really calls our house this early in the morning. She answered the phone, I let her know what the situation was and making light of my injuries, told her I would call her back as soon as we knew what hospital they would be taking me to.

The EMT's administered pain killers and started the drive to the hospital in Stony Plain, about a twenty minute drive from the accident scene. The drive was not by any means smooth, but with a second shot of morphine it became bearable. Finally we pulled into the emergency doors. They took me out of the ambulance into the emergency department.I didn't have to wait long in the hall before the doctor was there ordering x-rays and telling me that they would make me as comfortable as possible.

Pain was jolting through my body. The worst of it in my chest. Throughout it all I kept thanking Jesus for preserving my life, for allowing me to go through this and blessing me. Just after being x-rayed my wife and two of my daughters arrived, worry on their face, but gratitude in their hearts.

Upon examining the x-rays the doctor came back to inform us of the severity of the injuries. I had six fractures. Two vertebrae in my neck, my ankle, sternum, one rib and what I would find out later my right heal. My doctor consulted with the trauma unit at the university hospital in Edmonton. It was decided that they would stabilize me and transfer me to the trauma unit at the University hospital. Back into the ambulance and another half hour drive and into the trauma unit I was brought in for treatment and further assessment. It was a whole day from the time of the accident at 4:50 a.m. until my son-in-law arrived with my grandson who was 11 at the time at 4 p.m. I'll never forget the look on his face when he saw me. The tears as they rolled down his face. I motioned for him to come closer, when I was able to reach him I drew him in and hugged him, despite the pain, letting him know that I was alright and was going to be fine. This seemed to settle him down and made me feel better as well.

The following hours were filled with more x-rays and testing than I have ever been through in my lifetime. I was admitted, even though I kept asking if I could go home or when would I be able to go home. Five days passed in the hospital before being released. I was ready to go home with my wife who arrived to bring me home. During the days of recovery that lay ahead of us, my wife became my caregiver as I was unable to care for myself. Each morning she would take off the collar from around my neck as I lay motionless on the bed keeping my head still, according to the instructions given us by the doctors and nursing staff. During this time I noticed the care and love in my wife, a reflection of Christ's life in her, the patience that she showed gave me hope and encouragement. The healing process is still ongoing, but the joy and peace that accompany it has made it an experience that leaves me grateful for all the blessings arising from the experience. I know no matter what God is always there to help me through anything I face.

After four months I was able to return to work. I had to gradually work back up to full-time. Even today, ten months after the accident, I'm still not able to do everything I used to. Not long ago a fellow employee asked me how it was that through everything that happens in my life, and the life of my co-worker, how is it that we remain so happy, I could only give her an answer of, "It is our faith in God that gives us that joy and peace." It was a simple answer, but the truth!

In the bible there are many passages that give me hope one of my favourites is found in the book of the prophet Jeremiah, Chapter 29: 11-14 "For I know well the plans I have in mind for you, says the Lord, plans for your welfare, not your woe! Plans to give you a future full of hope. When you call me, when you go to pray to me, I will listen to you. When you look for me, you will find me. Yes, when you seek me with all your heart, you will find me with you says the Lord, and I will change your lot." For me this has been my strength and continues to be my strength. Each day as I travel with those whom I love and who love me, through the peaks and valleys, keeping our eyes on the prize we steadily go forward. I now am grateful for the life given me.

Debbie Franklin

Debbie Franklin is a successful entrepreneur, Wellness & Business Mentor, wife, mother, and "Grams." She is a Wellness & Business Mentor and International Best Selling Author (Superwoman Myths.) Debbie is city girl who lives on a small farm with her country boy husband and their English Cream Golden Retrievers, cat, horses, and cattle. She has a passion for helping women create a business they love, be more productive with their time, have focus, and get the support in their business, schedule, and life to allow them more freedom to do the things they love! Developing a business that you not only love, but also supports you can provide a harmonious home for your family. Debbie understands the role of being a mom (and a business woman) and how you are the "heart of your family.

Web: www.debbiefranklin.com

Email: contact@debbiefranklin.com

Facebook: www.facebook.com/thedebbiefranklin

Twitter: www.twitter.com/debbiefranklin

LinkedIn: www.linkedin.com/debbiefranklin55

Help Me: They're Not Listening!

I woke up that morning, knowing I was dying. My husband had left for work early that day. I got my two older children off to catch the bus to school, and then went back to bed. My three year old was playing next to the bed when all of a sudden I knew I was in trouble and needed help. I couldn't think straight and felt so disconnected, like I wasn't part of this world.

I called my mother-in-law and told her she needed to come get me and take me to the hospital. I couldn't function and was unable to care for my child. Luckily, she only lived a mile away and was there very quickly.

At the emergency room, the doctor came into the room and asked me what was going on. I knew I had one more chance for someone to help me or it would be too late. I silently prayed she would "hear" me.

I told her about a year ago, I had a hysterectomy at 35 and had been struggling ever since. They had immediately started me on hormones because I was still young. The first hormone they tried didn't help; all I did was cry. I was depressed, hardly able to function, and cried at everything. My doctor kept telling me it was the hormone changes, and I needed to be patient.

A few weeks later I was still struggling. I called the doctor and he switched me to a new hormone. This time I went from a weeping crying mess to raging angry person, who couldn't stand to be touched. My children would come up to me to put their arms around me and I would just cringe. It was all I could do not to cry out "don't touch me."

Again, I called my doctor, who at this point told me I needed to examine my marriage and my role as a mom. Obviously, I was having emotional problems and needed psychiatric help. He advised me this had nothing to do with my surgery and hormones, that I had other issues going on. I was desperate to feel better and so, I started therapy with a psychiatrist as advised.

The medications he put me on made me feel weird, out of touch, and all I wanted to do was sleep. My children were now helping me keep up the daily chores, as I couldn't function. My husband was gone working all day and doing all he could to support me, as we followed the doctors instructions. We were working on getting "me" back to normal.

On my next doctor visit, I told him how the medications were making me feel, so he added another medicine. I then started having severe panic attacks. Instead of looking at the different medications or the combination as giving me these side effects, he continually added medicines in order to counter act the side effects. I was a mess. I couldn't think straight enough to understand what was happening.

I was a strong independent woman, who had went back to school at the age of 32 to get her accounting degree, carried 15 hours of course work, President of Phi Theta

Kappa, did the bookkeeping and administrative work for our family business, took care of 3 children, and had a husband. I was now unable to take care of the house, my 10 year old daughter was managing the family, my husband was helping to take care of me, supporting me through my horrendous panic attacks, and we were helpless as to where to turn.

The day before ending up in the emergency room, I had gone to the psychiatrist again and explained how horrible I was doing. I wasn't me! I didn't feel like me, couldn't think straight, I was a nervous wreck, having at least one panic attack a day and some days, they were one right after another. His solution was to increase my medication.

I had talked to my mom that night and told her, I knew I was dying. I couldn't feel myself in the future. I felt like I was drowning and no one was around to help. The doctors weren't helping and no one else seemed to know what to do. I was lost and hopeless. Until....my mother in law took me to the emergency room and a female doctor walked into the room.

I poured out my story to that kind, gentle, wonderful doctor. She left the room telling me she would be back in a few minutes. She came back into the room, sat next to me on the table, put her arm around me, and opened the book she had with her. She proceeded to look up all the medicines the doctor had me on reading to me all the side effects. She then looked at me and said "I'm so sorry they have done this to you. I am surprised you are not dead. The good news is we are going to get you off of these, but the bad news is we have to do it slowly. These are strong medicines and we have to wean you off of them." She switched my hormones again that day and within a few days, I started to feel better. The little wheel in my stomach that felt like I was running all the time – stopped.

I was still having horrible panic attacks. I couldn't watch TV, listen to certain types of music, sugar or caffeine could set a panic attack in motion, and my body didn't understand the difference between being happy or excited and being anxious and scared.

I now had hope though. I had someone that had listened. I had someone that was working with me! I started researching and learning more and more about hormones, panic attacks, and was praying for God to direct me to the answers I needed to heal.

One evening after a particular bad day, I was down on my knees crying for God to bring me someone that could help me get over these panic attacks. They were debilitating and the medicines that helped me through them, had horrible rebound effects. The next day I was on edge, angry, and just felt like I was crawling out of my skin.

One day a friend that I hadn't talked to in years called. We were catching up on each other's lives and I told her what had been happening. She told me to check into an alternative form of health care. I had never heard of the method before, and I didn't know if I could find anything in our area.

I love how God works because the next day, I ran into someone that knew someone who taught the alternative health care in our area. I called to make an appointment to get in as soon as possible. I knew my prayers had been answered and I was on my way to back to myself.

My first appointment I learned due to the surgery, hormone changes, and medications I had been on, my sympathetic system was messed up. She would teach me how to regulate my breathing and be able to relax on cue. I had homework each day, which included listening to tapes on teaching me to breathe properly, and relaxation tapes that I had to do for 15 minutes, three times a day.

She also introduced me to Lavender essential oil. This oil is used widely used for its calming and relaxing qualities. I was still taking anti-anxiety medication and this would be helpful for me to use during my homework with the goal of not only balancing my system, but also not needing the anti-anxiety medicine anymore.

My body rebelled at first. I would try to relax and it would jump and panic. I would have do my breathing techniques and continually tell myself that I was safe and all would be ok. I was a quick learner and mastered the ability to calm my body when needed, but it took several weeks for me to feel "normal." The panic attacks came less frequently and became more anxiety, and then eventually went away.

It was 6 months after I was in the emergency room and finally had someone listen to me, that I felt stronger and more like my old self. It was then that I decided I needed to go back to my gynaecologist for my checkup.

When he came into the room, he looked at my chart and asked me why I hadn't come in sooner. It was past the time for my check up. I explained to him the last year and a half of hell I went through – all because he didn't listen to me.

I told him I had been going to him for over 12 years. He had delivered two of my babies. I asked him, in all that time, have I ever been over dramatic, ever been a "basket" case or ever seemed to him that I had such issues that I needed psychiatric care?

He simply replied, "No."

He then went on to apologize. He told me he should have listened to me and he should have known better. He explained that it was "rare" women had the problems I had experienced, but it did happen and again, he was very sorry I had gone through all that I had.

In talking to other women though, it is not "rare" and happens more frequently than I realized. I asked all the right questions before my surgery. I had heard that women stop desiring sex, gain weight, etc. after a hysterectomy. I was told they were all myths and there wasn't any basis to those concerns.

I gained 30 lbs. within 6 weeks after having my surgery. I was told that because I was lying around after surgery, not exercising etc. it was easy to gain weight. Really? Do you know how much food one would have to consume to gain that much weight?

I changed after my surgery. I was different. I told a friend that I had felt like a dog that had been spayed. I had lost my passion for life, my desire to have fun, and my whole perspective on life looked different.

That all changed though when I received the "right" hormones for me, learned alternative health care skills, and was introduced to essential oils. All these things started me on a journey to heal beyond my physical body. I found hope in a few minutes when a doctor was willing to take the time to really listen to me, and what I had been going through.

Don't go through what I did. Find a doctor that you trust and willing to build a working relationship with you BEFORE you need them. You are paying them for their knowledge and advise, but listen to your own body and what is best for you. If you prefer natural health solutions, make sure they are wiling to work with you.

After my experience, I set up an appointment to get to know a doctor before becoming a patient of theirs. I share what I went through and how important it is that we work together as a team. While, I respect their knowledge and opinion, I need them to work with me in respecting my decisions. I do not take any I medications, unless I cannot find a natural solution that works for me.

I am now proactive and focus on health care prevention vs. treatment. I no longer "blindly" follow any doctor's advice. I do my own research and work with them on finding solutions for healing my body.

I have empowered my family and myself with knowledge on how to support our body naturally through food, essential oils, and supplements that provide the body what it needs to heal naturally. Healing includes the body, mind, and spirit.

- Healthy food provides the body essential nutrients in order to function properly, while at the same time reducing dairy, sugar, gluten, GMO's and other toxic ingredients from your diet.

- Essential oils can support the different systems of the body naturally from supporting and boosting the immune system, providing emotional support, and making your own body care and cleaning solutions to reduce toxic chemical exposure.

- Managing stress with proper rest and incorporating practices, such as meditation has been shown to provide many health benefits.

- Exercise is also important in helping to condition the body, remove toxins, and reduce stress.

When dealing with a health issue or crisis, find someone that will listen. It is easier to be proactive in finding a doctor before you need them and establish a good relationship. Remember, you are in charge of your body, your health, and what is best for you.

Autumne Stirling

Autumne Stirling is a social worker with a background in child protection, emergency room trauma, mental health, concurrent disorders, and chronic pain. She is a survivor of childhood trauma and is an advocate for increasing awareness, understanding, and empathy for those experiencing mental health exceptionalities. She has struggled, and subsequently learned to thrive with Dissociative Identity Disorder, depression, anxiety, and self harm. Her passion has now turned to writing and this is her first publication. She intents to continue to share her story, along with the various traditional and non-traditional forms of treatment she continues to use in order to life an authentic, healing lifestyle.

Web: *http://www.strongwarriorhealing.com*

Email: *strongwarriorhealing@outlook.com*

Facebook: *facebook.com/autumnestirling*

Twitter: *twitter.com/autumnestirling*

Instagram: *autumnestirling*

Linked In: *www.linkedin.com/in/autumne-stirling-158300aa*

CHOOSING FAITH OVER FEAR:

PREGNANCY AFTER MULTIPLE LOSSES

My Stats:

Age: 38

Number of Children: 1 (age 7)

Total Number of Pregnancies: 6

Number of Miscarriages: 3

Number of Missed Abortions: 1

Currently: 35 weeks, 5 days pregnant

This fragment of my story is one that often makes others uncomfortable which is exactly what compels me to tell it. There is solitude in silence... a stillness. It is cold. Support comes with sharing. When one individual stands up and speaks up, pain can become empowering, purposeful, less isolating and can bring collective awareness. I have learned that speaking my truth helps me to feel more confident, less insecure and more connected to others. I feel that by sharing pieces of my life story, I can inspire hope and motivation in others. I believe that we each go through our own life tribulations and amid the hopelessness and suffering, we can come together, rise up and lift each other by being authentic and honest.

The topic of my chapter is "Pregnancy after Multiple

Losses," Choosing Faith over Fear. I very quickly and easily learned that pregnancy loss is quite a taboo subject in our society. It is seldom talked about, it is glossed over and there appears to be the fear that even uttering the words "miscarriage" or "still birth" will almost bring these tragedies into fruition. I believe the opposite. I believe that these things unfortunately happen quite frequently to families and that bringing these experiences and emotions to the table can only but offer healing, hope, camaraderie and relief for those affected. Here I am, doing my part.

I have a beautiful seven year old son. Although I experienced extreme hyperemesis gravidarum, my pregnancy was relatively smooth until I went into early labour at 29 weeks. Thankfully, my health care team was able to stop my contractions and I carried my gorgeous little boy until 39 weeks 6 days, with a good delivery. I had always just assumed that I would have two children. I was able to easily conceive my son and it never even crossed my mind that I would have difficulty with miscarriages, especially following a reasonably healthy pregnancy .

One year later I suffered through my first miscarriage. The grief, isolation, pain and fear that surrounded me during this time was unbelievable. I am a survivor of childhood trauma, but none of that pain or the strength I had built up from my healing of that trauma, had prepared me for the heartache of losing a child. I was also extremely unprepared for the lack of support I would receive. I was told on several occasions that I should "simply get over it," "put it behind me" or "my child was not actually a baby because it was an early loss." Several weeks went by and it felt like my social circle either forgot about the death of my child or that they did not wish to talk about it. If I brought it up, the subject was quickly changed or I would receive comments such as "Well at least you have one child," or "Lots of woman miscarry," or "At least your baby was not stillborn". Were these statements supposed to make me feel better? I felt alone, like I was "being hushed by society" and that I was making a big deal out, of essentially, a small event. It was an extremely isolating experience, my emotions shut down and I remember starting to feel absolutely nothing. Complete numbness took over. Instead of communicating, I shut down to everything and everyone, I was terrified of being hurt again and I was afraid to share my real emotions with anyone.

Following this loss, I had another miscarriage in my 2nd trimester, following by a missed abortion around twelve weeks. A missed abortion is when a baby passes away but the mother's body does not recognize the death, so one appears to be still pregnant. My baby had died at eight weeks, three days but, I found out my baby was no longer alive at my twelve week ultrasound. I required a D&C and my baby was cremated. Again, very few people in my life recognized this demise or provided me with the emotional support I required. I was extremely devastated by these losses and I found others began avoiding me as I was depressed, anxious and in deep grief. I felt completely hopeless and that I did not have the right to the feelings I was having. Very few people understood and I felt very little empathy from others. I was shocked that people told me I "was lucky enough to have one child and I should not be so upset, I should feel gratitude instead of grief." While I recognize I am very blessed to have a child, I feel that this did not take away the pain I was experiencing from losing numerous pregnancies. I'm not sure when we as a society decided it was okay to judge each others grief. I struggled to have the emotional energy and strength to parent my son. I was beyond depressed for years and felt incredible stress and guilt for being such an inadequate mother and person. Instead of having support and people around me to love and help me, I was condemned and criticized which ultimately led me to feel more shame and increased isolation. I hated myself for how I was feeling, but I was overwhelmingly buried in grief.

I was at the lowest point in my life and knew I needed to reach out. I began to actively engage in trauma and grief counselling which was different then just attending therapy. I became an active participant in my life. I was showing up again and again, which was a remarkable change. I journaled daily, I practiced the meditation and the breathing techniques I learned, instead of just expecting them to miraculously work. I did yoga every single day and became more skilled at living in the present moment. I took care of myself physically which meant not sleeping in and having a shower even when I did not feel like it. I ate. I went to bed at the same time and got up at the same time every day… even on the weekends. I took my medication faithfully. I called the crisis line if I needed to and got real with how I was truly feeling. I started being honest with myself. I set daily intentions in which I would empower and affirm my commitment to my healing. I started to forgive myself, I stopped blaming myself for feeling sad and I began to loving myself for all that I was, grieve and all.

Fast forward several years, I am divorced, I am parenting my son in all the ways I always knew I could and I am in an amazing, healthy relationship. I feel like I am able to freely communicate my feelings and I feel more love than I have in my entire life. My son has a wonderful relationship with my fiancé, which truly is the most important thing for me. On a trip to New Orleans, July 2015, we became pregnant and were very joyful about our new addition, only to miscarry our child when we were six weeks along. It was devastating. I thought that I would never be able to give my child a sibling and I felt like an absolute failure. I could feel myself losing faith. I felt inadequate as a partner. I felt like I had little to offer to anyone. After all my hard work, I was hitting that rock bottom hopeless space all over again. I knew I did not want to be here.

Thankfully, with the support of my significant other and the trauma therapy I have continued to faithfully engage in, I was able to move through this miscarriage much more smoothly than in the past and the feelings of hopelessness did not last long. I relied on the people in my life that were supportive and actively did not allow myself to become isolated. Although I felt the draw to emotionally detach, I stayed with my feelings and stopped fighting what I needed to feel. I journaled about my feelings and I was as creative as possible. I shared my story, which I believe is a huge part of recovery and grieving for me. I supported other woman that had experienced pregnancy loss and allowed myself to be emotionally vulnerable to them as well. I learned that I grieve best through mutual support and authenticity, with those I trust but additionally with strangers that have had similar experiences. I learned to no longer be afraid or ashamed of my truth.

Now here I sit, one year, five months later and we are pregnant again with a little girl! As I type this I am 25 weeks, 6 days pregnant and there are plenty of emotions that come along with this. Since the birth of my seven year old, I have never been this far along in a pregnancy, which is absolutely thrilling and exciting. I am full of gratitude. I have also had to learn to cope with a great deal of anxiety. The kind of anxiety that is not going anywhere anytime soon. It has been learning to be hopeful in a different type of way, which I have discovered is extremely interesting and life changing.

How do I choose faith over fear everyday, even when faced with incredible odds that everything may not result in the outcome I desire?

To say that this has not been a challenging time, would be

an understatement, however challenging does not equate hopeless, unmanageable or impossible. For me, I have used this time to deepen my spiritual connection, I have use meditation to decrease my stress and I have really tried to emotionally process and honestly share my true feelings. I have been able to verbalize and feel excitement about all my hopes and dreams for our daughter but also I have shared my fears, anxieties, my bodily discomforts and insecurities without shame or embarrassment. It has been a very freeing and liberating experience. I have felt my connection with my son and fiancé deepen and I have even allowed myself to emotionally bond with my daughter. This has been monumental step for me, especially to move through an emotionally and mentally difficult time coping in healthy, strong ways. For me, I currently define strength and health as me being able to feel the light and dark in all situations I face, but maintain healthy boundaries and positive coping mechanisms. I still have moments of tears, insecurities and fear, however, I no longer allow these moments to define me and I also do not dwell on these times. I openly allow myself to experience them, feel them and grow from them. I have learned that being honest with all that and accepting my truth has actually decreased my anxiety and improved my feelings of hopefulness. Embracing myself and my current situation as it is, all the wonderful things, the difficult realities and coming through to the other side have really opened up my ability to experience hope for all it can be. With all the grievous incidents I have been through, my faith has increased, allowing me to trust that there is a great plan for me and my family. As each day passes, my love for my family and myself grows and strengthens. My family is real and our bond is true. I have learned to trust my fiancé like I have never trusted before. It has been a process and I have had to face some difficult truths about myself along the way, however, this journey has put spark back into my life and hopefulness back into my soul.

Writing this has boosted my spirits and affirmed for me that I am on the perfect mental, emotional and spiritual path for me. My combined experiences have taught me to never give up hope because I can never be certain what has been planned for me. Assuming that the worst things will happen do absolutely nothing but bring my energy and resiliency down. Sure there will likely be disappointments and struggles, but that is all a part of it. Without these difficulties, I would never be able to see all the light and goodness in others and to feel authentic love. Hope sustains me.

As I conclude, we are 26 weeks pregnant and our daughter is about the size of a butternut squash. She just kicked me and it brings tears to my eye. Tears of joy, tears of love and tears of hope. The 14 week countdown is on and I simply cannot wait to look directly into the beautiful eyes of hope.

Janea Trapp

Janea Trapp serves as the Director of Health and Wellness Services with Ideal Health of Kansas located in Wichita, Kansas. She is also a certified coach, speaker and trainer with The John Maxwell Team. Her personal journey of weight loss and health coupled with her passion for personal growth allows her to connect with clients to maximize their results.

LinkedIn: www.linkedin.com/in/janeatrapp

Facebook: www.facebook.com/idealhealthofkansas

LIFE CHANGE IS LIFE CHANGING

It was late one Friday afternoon in December 2014, just before the end of the work week, when the words "perception is reality" cut like daggers in my heart. My supervisor, at the time, was delivering my annual review, and as he did so, a tidal wave of emotions flooded my mind. Wow? Is this really how my peers see me? Is he seriously telling me that all the issues within our group are related to my dissatisfaction with recent changes and MY attitude? What about everyone else's attitude? The whole experience was so surreal. Just two years prior, I was exceeding expectations in my current role, for the second year in a row; and today, I am hearing if I do not make significant improvements, my position with the company would be in jeopardy? I was informed that Human Resources expected that I be placed on a personal improvement plan, a form of professional rehabilitation if you will, addressing all my areas of improvement.

On the way home, I reflected on the past year and how much I struggled just to exist. I had been diagnosed with Hyperthyroidism in June 2012 and after choosing the Iodine 131 Ablation therapy to destroy all thyroid function I had to deal with Hypothyroidism. I really thought the health issues would be behind me once we corrected the dose of my Synthroid, unfortunately they were not. Although, I had not been specifically diagnosed with Chronic Fatigue Syndrome (CFS) I was being treated for its symptoms as sleep studies and other autoimmune disease tests could not pinpoint any other reason for the constant fatigue I felt. More frustrating than feeling constantly tired was the foggy disconnected feeling. The best way I can describe it is that sometimes the light was on and sometimes it just wasn't. I worked hard at managing my symptoms with additional rest; however, whenever I went more than one or two days without a good night's rest it became difficult to handle daily stresses of work and home. My doctor prescribed a medication that would help but my insurance carrier wanted me to try a step therapy approach before they would cover the medication as there was no generic form of the drug. I refused to take the stimulant up until the moment when it was apparent that I was not managing the symptoms well enough at work. It was brought to my attention that at times I was real engaged and making progress on projects and daily activities only to seem to withdrawal and struggle the next. Then "miraculously" (that was the term my supervisor used) I would be reengaged. My work was no longer consistent and I could not be counted on. So, I started taking a drug that helped with symptoms but was not intended to treat the underlying medical condition. The stimulant kept me awake and alert but it also caused me to become easily irritated and moody.

Everything was finally crumbling down around me. My life was like a house built on sandy soil, rather than solid ground, and the tide had finally come in to wash it away. Later that night I remember looking into the mirror and all I saw was a broken individual. I no longer recognized myself. Where did I go wrong? I wanted to achieve all these preconceived goals that I believed were within my reach if I just kept pushing myself harder and volunteering for projects no one else on our team wanted. The only problem was I had to be able to maintain these projects along with a piece of everything else. I knew that I was capable of so much more than my current day to day activities and yet all my efforts to learn and grow were expected to fit within a 40 hour work week. Let's face it, my attitude was what is was because I was burnt out. The fire that was once lit inside me began to dim. It became easy to fall prey to advice or views of those around me. Words such as, "I don't know why you push yourself so hard, you will not be compensated for it; or, you will never be allowed to become anything more than that group allows you to be." I think I finally realized that I was no longer in a role that challenged me or inspired me to be my best. I had a supervisor that I no longer trusted and along the way I had lost hope and the belief in myself that I could even make a difference. The only question now was, how I expected to dig out of the hole I dug for myself. I was in need of some serious guidance.

With my hands folded tightly and tears running down my cheeks I prayed. "Heavenly Father, I've made such a mess out of things. I've put this job ahead of my family just trying to advance or to make more money, and for what? I have nothing to show for it. Maybe my husband is right, I will never be anything more than what they allow me to be. There is so much resentment and anger in my heart that I am not sure if I can recover. The only things I am sure about is that I am not the wife my husband deserves me to be; I am not the mother my little boy needs me to be; and most importantly, I am not the daughter you created me to be. You know there's a desire in my heart to be more and do more. Would you have placed it there if it wasn't meant to be? I just don't understand. Help me to understand. All I feel is guilt and shame. Please help me..." I fell asleep that night and the next morning there was actually a peace that had fallen over me. As I brushed my teeth I looked in the mirror and said out loud to myself, "I got this, it's time to loosen the reigns and follow God's lead. I HAVE a choice. I can be the individual they perceive me to be; or, I can work each day to become the person I want them to see. It's entirely up to me."

It was that December, that I began devoting at least an hour each evening to reading or engaging in some other form of personal improvement plan. I drafted that personal development plan and although I submitted it in mid-December as instructed, my supervisor did not get around to getting HR's approval until sometime in March of the following year. No matter, I was well on my way...I read a number of books, listened to audio books, and paid to attend workshops. I also began to build a better relationship with God. Sure, I prayed; but I would also just talk to Him. Sometimes on the drive to work or the way home in the evenings. I told him no matter what, I would trust in Him and I would follow his lead. There was a few items from my annual review that never set well with me. One day, in a team meeting, we were discussing Humility. I felt a nudge on my shoulder and an incredible urge to open my mouth and say something. I fought the feeling, but finally gave in. I remember asking my supervisor if it would be alright for me to discuss my last review to which he replied, "I don't know what you plan to say about it." I remember saying something like, "Last December, when I received my review I received a lot of feedback about how others perceived me. I want to apologize if I have ever done anything to make any of you feel discounted or uncomfortable coming to me for help..." That was the day I released myself from the shame I had felt from my review and in the long run, it strengthened my relationships with other members of the team.

My transformation was well on its way. I was repairing and building relationships and for the first time, instead of worrying about what was in it for me and my career, I began focusing on helping other members of the team with their projects and interests. As the weeks went on, I found myself developing a love for reading and personal growth. Routine meetings with my supervisor as part of my personal improvement plan were not being kept and I began to feel that he just didn't care. I found myself starting to really question his leadership. He was an alright manager, managing the day to day, but was he a good example of a leader? Why did I disagree with him on so many levels? I no longer trusted that he cared or had a vested interest in my personal growth and development so I decided to seek out other mentors. I prayed on it and my prayers were answered once again when I was able to enroll in a leadership certification program. Finally, I was able to surround myself and network with many like-minded individuals.

In July, my supervisor moved onto another role within an affiliated company and they promoted one of my coworkers to Team Lead. If it wasn't for this individual, I don't think that I would have survived my so called "professional probation". He met with me on a regular basis providing me with encouragement and the feedback I needed to keep moving forward. To, Dan, I will be forever grateful. I could breathe again. He listened and embrace my ideas and challenged my thinking in ways that made me better. Prior to his move, that December review was revisited and revised by my former supervisor detailing my successes and releasing me from the personal improvement plan.

Looking back I can tell you that 2015 was a year of

personal growth and awareness for me and at its very core was always a sense of hope. I had faith in knowing if I let God take the wheel that opportunities would present themselves to me. I may have lost faith in myself, but I never lost faith in God and His love for me. They say things are at their darkest just before the dawn. My situation was a lot like that. My career and family life in shambles one day and the next day came the dawn of a whole new perspective. Allowing God's hand to be at work each day of my life and not only seeking Him in my times of struggle. I would possess an attitude of gratitude and thank Him each day for His graces.

I would not be the individual I am today without that defining moment in my life. The review that left me feeling ashamed and bitter was a wake-up call to a bigger purpose for me. It led me down a path of personal improvement, seeking resources that I would have never sought had it not been for that Friday afternoon in December. I believed I was meant for something more and I held on to the hope that I would someday realize it. My life is much different today, but it didn't just improve over night. It took a lot of patience, daily prayer and of course, hope.

It is so easy to get caught up in the day to day of things. We envision our lives a particular way and we hold onto the vision so tightly we lose sight of who we are or what we are truly meant to do with our lives. I have found that when we deny God's presence and we go about our day to day attempting to achieve these well thought out plans, the bumps in the road, the challenges we face, might just be God's way of redirecting your course. Though the journey to where I am today was painful at times, I am grateful. My relationship with God is the strongest it has ever been and I am blessed beyond measure to have the love and support of my family and friends.

Back in January of 2015 I made a commitment to my health. I was a size 18 and had put on 60 pounds as a result of thyroid disease and the subsequent chronic fatigue. With the help of a health program and weight loss coach, I have dropped 70 pounds and went from the size 18 to a current size 8. I feel strong and have more energy than I have in a long time. It's funny how things work out sometimes. I have struggled with my weight for most of my life. I have felt ashamed and have missed out on opportunities and social engagements because of my embarrassment. When I was asked to be part of a local commercial for my weight loss clinic I was ecstatic, so proud of my accomplishment. When a coworker saw the commercial, he congratulated me on my success and told me how brave he thought I was to do the commercial. I hadn't thought about it being brave. Was I brave? It was just a local commercial that most of my coworkers hadn't come across. Oh, but how I wanted to be brave. I wanted other individuals struggling with their weight or health issues in general to know there is hope.

My weight loss success, along with my love of personal development, eventually opened the door to what I believe is my calling. To assist and empower other women, and men, to achieve their health and wellness goals. I said goodbye to my employer of 9 ½ years, taking a pay cut and less benefits that I had grown accustomed to, to become a weight loss and wellness coach. I have a newfound passion and hope burning inside of me to help and serve others. My hope is to be so transparent with my professional and personal experiences that I am able to help empower other individuals and instill hope in them that anything is possible because THEY have the power to make things possible. YOU have the power to make your hopes and dreams possible!

There is a reason why flight attendants instruct you to place and secure your oxygen mask first before aiding any small children or passengers seated next to you. We truly cannot be the blessing we want to be in the lives of others if we first do not love and take care of ourselves. John C. Maxwell often says, "You cannot give to others what you do not have to give." For each of us to add value to others we must first seek to add value to ourselves. If you are in a situation where your hopes and dreams are not supported, know that you are not alone. Seek out mentors that can offer advice, hold you accountable and above all encourage you in times when you need it most. Know that you are in control of your dreams and personal growth. Read something positive or say something you are grateful for out loud every day. Practice an "Attitude of Gratitude" and you will be amazed how quickly your outlook will change.

This is what I know…there is no way to measure the

amount of hope and conviction within an individual that has a dream and a willingness to work toward that dream. Just as there is no number on a scale or measuring tape that can quantify your self-worth or the value you contribute in the lives of others. Perhaps as you are reading this you feel you have lost hope. Here's the thing, it's not lost. Hope may be dampened at times or out of reach; but it is never lost. Just as the sun will rise in the morning, promising a new day, hope resounds with each beat of your heart. Love yourself and extend that love to others. You will be amazed at the changes you will discover in yourself and just maybe a bit surprised by the doors that will open to you.

Brenda Young

Brenda Young is a best-selling author, healing/meditation practitioner and empowerment coach. While Christian, she is a bridge to all cultures embracing Love, Peace and Wellness.

THE ROAD FROM GUTS TO GLORY

"Thy word is a lamp unto my feet and a light unto my path." Psalm 105

There IS a light shining in the darkness as in Psalm 105. But one day, my hope light went out. I was alone in the abyss. My prideful path looked rosy by day but led to a dark night of the soul with no hope in sight. Still, I defiantly went my own way, I knew better.

It proved difficult and dangerous. I was searching in all the wrong places. That road didn't lead anywhere but struggle, heartache and a dead end.

In the end, only God's Truth walks me home. But I needed to stop seeking and awake to the surety that I am already found in Christ.

Whatever challenge you're struggling with, I guarantee that God is cracking you open like a mustard seed to shine His HOPE Light in. No matter how dire your situation, He will break through your blindness and hopelessness – until the pain turns into PRAISE.

But that's not my whole story. I wasn't always this faithful. I was a master of hopelessness! My heart was wounded and my mind was occupied with doubt and fear of how I would survive in this world.

I was a prisoner dragging a massive ball and chain of pain. Abandonment, rejection, and violation - they all had a grip on me - and my heart.

Those binds sent me to ER one night with blood pressure off the charts. It was a healing crisis. In a lineage of heart disease and family bondage, my heart spoke up. It was enslaved. My heart pumped wildly throughout my difficult life. It contracted through my disappointments and traumas. It pounded through my guilt, shame and blame. It had enough!

My heart wasn't free. It was held in hopelessness. And that night, the enzymes in my blood told the story, indicating either a stroke or brain bleeding. My heart said: STOP! But God said, "I'm purifying you."

I prayed all night before my CT scan. As my head entered the machine the next morning, I felt the Holy Spirit's presence. I knew I had to surrender to Him completely for the Miracle Maker to do His work.

Thankfully, inviting God into my troubled heart to purify my toxic blood worked! My tests were fine and I was released that day.

"He healeth the broken in heart, and bindeth up their wounds."

~ Psalm 147.3

When I faithfully asked God to heal my wounds, He opened me wider, deeper and more powerfully by His Healing Hand. Praise God!

Shortly after I got out of the hospital, I had another big challenge: a relationship breakup.

It wasn't only one severed connection that shook me. It was all of them. It was my steady stream of men whom I constantly sought acceptance from because something deep inside me was thirsty for real freedom.

And it hit on some trauma from my teens when I was violated. Did I feel insecure? Desperate? Hopeless? You bet! My hope light, my sparkle had not only dimmed. It was gone.

I experienced too much emptiness and broken-heartedness. I was deeply unfulfilled and even though I love my family, many times I just wanted my life to end. It was far too painful, and I didn't seem to fit in anywhere. Deep down, I craved more of God's Love and less rejection from the world, so I kept veering off with my hidden chains and wounded heart.

Beyond all the relationship calamities, I experienced deep poverty, without a home, husband, vehicle or any work at a mature age. For a time, I went to food banks, received generous donations from family and friends, and found places to live where I didn't pay rent. I was captive.

I couldn't deny the cycle of dishonor that had punctuated my life. But what was I honoring? Whom was I adoring and putting my faith, hope and trust into? Other people! And 'awakened consciousness' that never delivered but only unpeeled more dysfunction.

As long as I went 'my own way', there was no way my life was going to drastically improve. By seeking oneness through world culture, I gained autonomy but lost my authenticity – the real liberated life God designed for me - until my soul cried out for God's Authority.

My way led to poverty. God's way is Abundant.

"For what is a man profited, if he shall gain the whole world, and lose his own soul" or "what shall a man give in exchange for his soul?" ~ Matthew 16:26

That's why we become hopeless. We deny God and ourselves because we're living a lie. We're in a stronghold. It's a dark hole that leads nowhere. It's not the path of Light that God wanted for me.

He has much more in store! He wants to take us deeper than our strong willed feet wander on a downward spiral of suffering, regret and defeat.

He wants us Victorious.

"For as the heavens are higher than the earth, so are my ways higher than your ways, and my thoughts than your thoughts. ~ Isaiah 55.9

It's exhausting to keep giving and still feel bankrupt. My soul was desperate to return home to Christ – for something satisfying, authentic and enduring. I yearned for my life to be free and walk upright again.

"Blessed are they which do hunger and thirst after righteousness, for they will be filled." ~ Matthew 5.6

Through God's Grace (also my Mom's name, born of my Grandmother Mary) I kept coming back to church, bruised, battered and broken humbly dragging my chains behind me. It was hell for too long. I held onto people, places and events that hurt me. I was drowning. But Our Savior held out a hand. I stopped trying to bail out my life, and simply said 'Yes Lord. I am Yours'!

Finding real hope is discovering the most magnificent treasure. I no longer need to hide because the truth is plain to see. It sets me free.

God reveals His freedom and truth in mysterious ways. For me, it started with a Bible study workbook called Breaking Free by Beth Moore, gifted by my church friend Penny. Bless her soul for knowing then what I didn't: Beth's book would profoundly change my life one day by calling me back to the Bible.

Liberty was available all along on my bookshelf. Like

Christ, that book sat patiently waiting for me. But I wasn't ready. Life had to get so painful for me to admit that my garden tending was not producing good fruits. Jesus knocked on my garden gate, but I had to open from the inside.

One day at church, I did open my heart wide. Yes, my heart was torn and bleeding, but I tearfully sang it out expanding past my raw edges. Later, my pastor spoke the familiar scripture in John 4:18 of the Samarian woman at the well having had 'five husbands and living with a man she was not married to'.

I later went to our prayer team and confessed, sobbing: I was that woman: the gypsy; the wanderer; the lost pilgrim; and the one who could not commit my soul fully to Christ, because I didn't feel worthy. I felt forsaken. Surely – I believed - I was fatally flawed and unacceptable, or my life would not be the shambles it was.

I was in a massive fight with God - with the masculine - for the time I was violated and the world went wrong. I was in a fight with my father who was an alcoholic when our family split up. I was in a fight with the men who left me, the people who rejected me – and with a Father in Heaven whom I felt abandoned me to an alien, hostile planet.

I was captive in the ruins of ancestral sin. Once a crop is tainted, that poisonous seed carries throughout lineages. The deceiver was suffocating me in an ancient cycle of blame, shame and insecurity – until I refused to be a victim.

But God makes beauty from ashes when we ask Our Redeemer for freedom through forgiveness. He loosened me and burned the foul crop – to cut me from my past - to reveal HIS legacy for me.

"The lines are fallen unto me in pleasant places; yea, I have a goodly heritage." ~ Psalm 16.6

In that moment of truth, I knew God wanted me to FULLY surrender my cup to Christ – into the Living Water, instead of the wrong fountains where I would always be parched.

As Break Free author Beth Moore states, "God is my only guarantee."

"For whomever drinketh from the water that I shall give him shall never thirst, but the water that I shall give him shall be in him a well of water springing up into everlasting life." ~ John 4:14

God can't fill our insatiable thirst without accepting Jesus as Redeemer. He's the only freedom font I know. We can't find water in the desert of our own desires. It's a hopeless wasteland. God showed me the way from pain to promise, and now to praise.

"As for God, His way is perfect: the word of the LORD is tried: he is a buckler to all those that trust in Him." ~ Psalm 18:30

Only God can sever our strongholds and renew our

strength. There are no deficiencies with Him. The inequities are in us. We're HopeFULL when we surrender wholeheartedly to His Absoluteness.

Every time I resisted God's purpose for my life, I lost His Powerful Presence. I choose death over life attracting hell over Heaven.

Many people have tasted freedom and fell off the path again and again. I did. I forgot that with God dwelling in us, there is no lack. All things are possible!

Whenever I slipped away, it was my pride. I knew better. It always led to disillusionment, division, and destruction. Really, I crucified myself.

But there's a rock at 'rock bottom' and that is the faithfulness of Christ. He died for us as savior but He lives in us as liberator. And He reaches out to us constantly, especially when we're in trouble.

I'm lucky to get out of the shadow of death alive. That valley may have appeared to have milk and honey, but it had a dark root. It took from me. It confused me. It physically challenged me. It was like a threatening sword at my neck.

But our Almighty Wise King is so much greater than what I trod through. He turned my danger into gain with an opportunity to testify His truth: God conquers all and the blood of Christ redeems.

But we have to ask for help. I'm so grateful I did!

God snapped my most stubborn chain with His Word. On silken pages, His Voice reached me through time eternal. And I KNEW it was true: God became Christ for us – to free us from sin, from our own wayward ideas that we think are superior but never can be. We're not God.

"I am the LORD: that is my name: and my glory will I not give to another, neither praise to graven images." ~ Isaiah 42.8

By our Father in Heaven, Christ gave us the greatest gift we'll ever receive: Eternal Life. Thank you Jesus for redemption.

Now I am vibrantly alive and anchored in God's truth. And I am here to tell you. There is no one else but God. And He lives in us through Jesus Christ. Step out of your hopeless shadow and into His light and might. There is no battle too big for Him. He's here for you!

Anchoring God's eternal love and everlasting hope light means leaving my stubborn ways behind. It's being 'raw for God'. It takes guts to get to the glory, as author Beth Moore says.

It takes courage to come fully clean, to butt up against the truth that sets us free. When we're broken and laid bare, we're cast into the Holy Fire for purification at our core. We're on the threshing floor, ready to be reborn or cast away.

"For they have sewn the wind, and they shall reap the whirlwind: it hath no stalk: the bud shall yield no meal: if so be it yield, the strangers shall swallow it up." ~ Hosea 8:7

God wants us purified and on fire for Him! He wants us glorious!

But I had to see the vice-grip I was in and seek forgiveness. It's humbling to kneel and pray: 'I'm sorry. Please forgive me.' And it's hard to let go if we don't know who or what will catch you. But God did when I fully surrendered and opened my heart to Him.

But our hearts, made for beauty, can be wicked fraudsters when we take our eyes off God's glorious promise. There's a price to pay when we substitute the real for the false, the temporary for the eternal, and idols for Christ alone. That price is captivity. And if you don't think our world is captive, look around.

But Our God is Greater. Everlasting Praise! Christ has paid our ransom!

Christ's blood continues to remove my stains and restores my soul. I pray to become white as the snow of His garment! Do you know any manmade product that can do that? I don't!

When the thunder and lightening of God's Perfect Love rumbled through my tumbled life, it was complete chaos. It was traumatic. It was a total loss of control. But then, divine order, unimaginable joy and profound peace entered after the storm.

When I look back, I have to laugh at myself! In my new age, crystal carrying, card flipping hippy life, I prophesized that 'Christ consciousness' would reset our world. Well, how am I supposed to embrace the consciousness of Christ if I'm not in relationship with Him?

I kept putting my faith where it didn't belong – outside Jesus. Yet there is no other One who can give us the kind of love, acceptance and security our soul deeply craves but our Loving Parent living in us through His Son.

If you're hopeful for 'the perfect life' to appear on the outside, turn inwards. God works from the inside out.

Reach IN to Him. Cry in anger, frustration or desperation. Throw a pillow! Do what you must, but call on Him. God is a Good Father! He wants our best. He wants to renew us, to keep His Love alive in our hearts 'as a lantern' in His Holy Name.

Praying to God and welcoming Christ into my heart is so worth it! I have been able to move mountains of hopelessness into constant joy even in my pain. This world cannot satisfy, and I know it. Christ has become my light, my strength and my song. It's Amazing Love!

"Thou wilt show me the path of life: in thy presence is fullness of joy; at thy right hand there are pleasures for evermore." ~ Psalm 16.11

God is all I want. Christ is all I ever needed. God's grace is above diamonds – anything this world can offer. He never intended us to be slaves of our misguided lives but servants of His peace.

Once you experience God's overflowing indescribable love, abundant joy and impermeable strength, your only song will be one of PRAISE. He becomes so ALIVE in you. You'll see Him everywhere and in everything. You'll want to bless everyone who crosses your path. You'll want to stand on the rooftops and shout: "YES LORD! I am Yours!"

And best of all, you won't have one iota of concern what other people think of your exuberance – because His Love is contagious!

"The Heavens declare the glory of God; and the firmament showeth his handiwork." ~ Psalm 19

There's HOPE in the storm. There's FREEDOM in my story. If you feel exempt, trust me, God is pursuing you all the time.

His devotion is a boundless sea; He perpetually pulls us toward Him in a loving encounter. His Promise, His Word fulfills: to deliver 'the peace which passeth all understanding' – to carry us from the bonds of hopelessness to freedom.

How can I absolutely know God is powerfully working to break every chain in my life and can in yours? Because He is! No matter what the problem, my HOPE is in the Lord. My life is secure in God's hands.

Whatever you're doing, wherever you've roamed: distracted, discouraged or disempowered, God is here now. Exalt Him. Ask for help.

His powerful name stands above all and resounds forever. Trade your hopeless sorrow for the fullness of His freedom and glory!

You don't need to rely on stocks, lottery luck or wish upon a star. God's promise is unshakeable. Invite His love in to surround you and bring His WORTH into your life. I promise you. It will be sweeter!

"The fear of the LORD is clean, enduring forever; the judgments of the LORD are true and righteous altogether. More to be desired are they than gold, yea, than much fine gold: sweeter also than honey and the honeycomb. ~ Psalm 19: 9,10

God's love IS gold.

When I think of how I used to shut the bible when I read fear and judgment references, it now makes me sad. But I understand. I experienced the fear God talks about. Instead of using it against me, He used it as a lever to heal my broken life and declare my freedom!

His judgment is now my discernment that if the things I desire aren't God's Desire, I'm going to let them go or get hurt again and again. I don't have to be hopeless now, because my faith is renewed!

The more I trust and pray, the stronger He is in me. Because I now worry less, I have more room to be inspired – and more time to translate my inspiration into 'inspire-action'!

I know that if I didn't surrender when I did, I would still be a prisoner of my own free will. But it wasn't free at all. I paid a big price, and so did my loved ones who suffered with me.

While I was sinful, shameful, and brokenhearted, they were grieving for me. But no one could help. Only Christ can. And whether you call it sin or not, I missed the mark big time!

But How God loves when we turn to Him! There IS hope for the hopeless, grace and forgiveness, mercy and healing for each one of us, as Third Day so eloquently sings.

If you feel like the world is weighing upon you, cry out to Jesus. I'm elated that I did! I am free in Him.

"STAND FAST therefore in the liberty wherewith Christ hath made us free, and be not entangled again with the yoke of bondage." ~ Galatians 5.1.

God wants to permanently loose our tethers. He wants to forever lift us from pain into His Eternal Land of Promise – to be in Communion with us through Christ. Say YES.

When God finally sets your heart free, an amazing thing happens: Your soul catches fire! You embody unfathomable joy! You are so thankful to finally be free; all you want to do is glorify God!

When you fully open the floodgates of your heart to him, your life becomes filled with new passion, power and purpose. You are unstoppable. Hopelessness becomes a thing of the past. You'll want more and more of Him! Best of all, you are at PEACE.

Miracles continue to fill my life, like precious gold in those broken crevices of despair that used to paralyze me. The Holy Spirit now moves me more potently and passionately than ever before into Service.

I long for God's embrace to hold my life each moment. I am in total surrender to His Love; He keeps revealing more of His Glory to me.

The Lord is the Shepherd of my New Life. When life does present another significant challenge, I am strong in Christ. I am free in God's Promise. I am no longer bound.

Let the power of God's Infinite Love draw you near. Abide in Him. Let His Mighty Hand nourish, lift and liberate you!

"Abide in me, and I in you. As the branch cannot bear fruit of itself, except it abide in the vine; no more can ye, except ye abide in me." ~ John 15.4

God's Perfect Love never fails. Let Christ be the one we seek when all else comes crashing. His HOPE endures forever. Glory in the Highest.

I give God the last hopeful word:

"Behold, I will do a new thing; now it shall spring forth; shall ye not know it? I will even make a way in the wilderness, and rivers in the desert." ~ Isaiah 43.19.

Mofoluwaso Ilevbare

Mofoluwaso Ilevbare is a Confidence Coach for Career Women, an International Speaker, Trainer & a Women Empowerment Advocate. Her passion is to inspire and enable women to DISCOVER, DEVELOP, and DELIVER their God-given talents so they are super confident at work and happier in life.

She is positively contagious and delivers her message of hope, confidence, and fulfilling purpose through 1:1 & group coaching, key note speeches, lunch & learns and workshops.

For speaking engagements / coaching, you can reach her :

Web: *www.mofoluwasoilevbare.com*
Facebook: *facebook.com/mofoluwasoilevbare*
Instagram @ *growyourconfidence_forsuccess*
LinkedIn: *ch.linkedin.com/in/mofoluwasoilevbare*
Her not-for-profit organisations: *www.wcbpurpose.org ; womeninspiringwomenng.com*

THE PINK LINE

My mum got married at 22. At 29, she had given birth to four beautiful girls, her pride and joy. By the time she was 31, she had lost all the pregnancy weight and looked like she never even got married. So, as you can imagine, I grew up seeing my mum looking young and vibrant. In my teenage years, going out together with my sisters and my mum was fun- we all dressed alike and looked alike. Sometimes, she even got mistaken as a sister and not our mum. I loved her physique and the idea of having kids early. and I dreamt it would happen for me exactly the same way.

Well, one part of it did. I met my charming prince at an early age and by the time I got to my first year of college, we were already committed to building a lasting future together. Six months after my graduation, we got married. I was 22 going on 23. Not bad for my dream, right?

We decided not to have kids in our first year - it gave us time to know one another better, travel around the world together and simply enjoy being a couple. It was fun but also a risky thing to do because we knew that in our African culture, once you get married, family and societal expectations set in. Many people expect to hear baby news in nine month's time. It's very common to see strangers staring at your tummy three to four months after you get married hoping to see a baby bump. Family members may make some insinuations in conversations and if nothing shows in twelve months, you may be having a conversation.

Well, for those who cared enough to ask, we simply explained it was by choice. As time went on, and we felt we were ready to welcome a third party in our home and take care of him/her, we prayed and trusted God I would get pregnant in no time. The second year passed by and so did the third, but what could be happening? Now, the pressure was mounting and we had run out of excuses or explanations to give. The ecstasy of flirting and romance now got mixed up with desperation for conception. I lost count of the number of pregnancy home kits I bought and tested month after month hoping to see the pink line. "Oh, God", I cried out many times. "This can't be happening to us. Please do something. Work a miracle." Many days, I would cry and cry. Then, I would wipe my tears and put on a happy face like everything was going on well but deep within, my heart melted every time I saw a little baby, my heart skipped a beat whenever my period was late by a day, and my hope was shattered overtime the results showed no sign of the pink line.

At some point, we sought medical help. Thank God for doctors, although they can be a pain in your butt sometimes. So much grammar trying to explain the different medical conditions and scenarios, many times with a straight face like it is what it is. What followed were a series of tests, tons of needle pricking, and laboratory test results. Some tests were more painful than others but on many occasions, the psychological pain surpassed the physical one. There were days I found it so hard to cope with the emotional strain I felt. Yet, I had to show up at work as usual, perform my roles impeccably, juggle that with and in my ministry like everything was okay.

One day, while cleaning up my room, I found a little green book hidden in between a pile of old shoes. It turned out to be my very first journal. I kept this journal during my college years and inside it were many memories, prayers, thoughts, inspired poems, and names of people who had made a great impact in my life. Flipping through it, I came across a particular page. It was an inspired writing I had written in the wee hours of the morning that day. I must have woken up from sleep to write it. It was titled " Strength to Conceive". The basic message was centred around the story of Sarah, Abraham's wife, as told in the Bible, who for 90 years was barren and without a child. One day, while they entertained three guests, supposedly angels, one of them said to Abraham "By this time next year, Sarah your wife will bear a child". Sarah heard these words and laughed sarcastically but quietly. I could imagine her saying "What a joke! After how many years?" Please do not scam me - I'm too old for that." Yet, the angel asked her to believe. What a test of faith! Coming back to my journal, I must have pondered over the story for a while and written down the following words:

By faith Sarah herself also received strength to conceive a seed

She bore a child even when she was past the age

It could only happen because she believed
And judged Him faithful, who had promised.

Through faith, strength comes to conceive
Through faith, strength comes to receive
Through faith, strength comes to endure
Through faith, strength comes to push through

With the many so-called impossible dreams
Which lay in our path daily
The problems that stay past midnight
The darkness of the future clouding our view

If only we had just a little faith
small it might be, just like the mustard seed
then maybe we can soar above the mountains
Mounting higher on the wings of faith
Even when the way ahead seems so dim
Taking the Guardian's unchanging hand
His word is true - and can't be faulted
He's ever faithful no matter what

If only we had just a little faith
Small it might be just like the mustard seed
Then maybe we'd join the league of the faithful
And sit together with Mother Sarah
Who brought forth what man had thought impossible

Step out in faith and bring forth
Yes, bring forth all God has placed inside of you
For by faith Sarah received strength to conceive
And bore a son she called "Laughter"
God longs to fill our mouths with laughter

If only we find the strength to believe.

The tears filled my weary eyes as I read the words over and over again. Despite writing the words five years ago, it jumped out at me like it was just written yesterday. How did God know this day would come? Was this His way of preparing me for the long wait we were having so far? If He knew all along, then this must mean that He is with me even now.

That moment, I caught a new revelation. I could envision the future. I closed my eyes and I could picture the sun about to shine somewhere behind the grey clouds. "No more tears." I said to myself. "This is it!". I have cried my last tear. It's time to believe again, dream again, try again and pray again.

When hope rises in your heart, you find the strength to try again. When hope rises in your heart, you begin to see things differently than you did before.

I didn't notice I had knelt down in the process. So, I got up, wiped my tears, determined to look at my present situation with a different set of lenses. The next few months were hectic and very busy for me at work. I was part of a team responsible for a major product launch that would help more lower class women and girls afford sanitary towels so they could be free to go to school or get jobs without the fear of blood stains.

Finally, the product launch date arrived. The president of the country was our special guest of honour. Everything had to go as planned. The team worked tirelessly to deliver a world-class event. Finally, five hours later, we could breath a sigh of relief. The event went extremely well, the guest entourage was so impressed and we had waved our goodbyes to the presidential convoy as they exited from the venue. I couldn't wait to get out of my brown leopard-skinned high heel shoes. On my way to the rest room, I passed by a friend to say hello. We spent some time debriefing about the event and expressing gratitude that everything went well. Then it happened.

I could hear voices calling my name but they seemed so distant. Gradually, I tried to move my mouth to respond to my name and struggled to open my eyes. "What was going on?" I asked myself quietly as I tried to open my eyes to the reality that was in front of me. The last thing I could remember was laughing frantically with my colleague. Now here I was lying on the stretcher placed strategically on the floor of the clinic. I felt wet and it was strange seeing a few people leaning over me calling my name, checking my pulse, wondering if I was conscious. I tried to get up but no one would let me. I finally found my voice and I asked "What's going on? What happened to me?." "You suddenly slumped and I got very scared." said my friend. "Probably it may be due to the exhaustion from your just concluded event. We'll have to take you to the hospital for some tests."

So what started on a high note wasn't going so well

anymore. Off I went in the ambulance to the hospital to get some tests done. I felt okay but it was better to take the precautions. Whatever happens, I was sure I would have to take a few days off to recover from the strenuous planning of the last few months. I got some blood tests done, got some aspirins, and was discharged to go home. The next day, I went back for my test results and doctor's consultation. Thank God, everything was fine- I was probably fatigued and low on sugar. As I heaved a sigh of relief and picked up my bag to leave, the doctor said "I'd like you to take a pregnancy test!" Did I just hear that? You must be kidding me. "I haven't taken one of those in a very long time." I said to him. "Why should I do it now?" I asked. One voice in my head said "What do you have to lose?" Another voice in my head said "Don't get your hopes up. " The doctor felt my blood tests results were a little unusual but before giving me any further drugs, he wanted to be sure I wasn't pregnant.

I took the test with my heart in my mouth still battling with the two conflicting voices in my head. A third voice joined in and said " What if you're pregnant? That would be the biggest miracle in history!" The results were instant-indeed I WAS PREGNANT!!

I couldn't breath. Could this be happening? For real? At the most unexpected moment? You see, I had put my heart so much at ease that it would happen whenever God says it will that somehow I had suppressed the worry and the anticipation and gone on enjoying my life, keeping myself busy with the things in life that mattered to me. It reminds me of the disciples who were praying for Peter's release (who had been thrown in prison) but refused to believe that God could have answered the prayer so quickly when Peter finally showed up at the door.

The following day, I had a proper scan done - the verdict was in. After 5 years in waiting, I was 8 weeks pregnant and I didn't even know it. The doctors said our chances were very slim without some major intervention but here I was, touched by the mighty Doctor himself.

Today, we are blessed with two supernatural miracles, the first after five years of waiting, the second after another six years of waiting. The sound of their voices echoing around the house as they call me "Momma" makes all the years of waiting melt away.

Perhaps as you read this, you are currently in the "waiting room of life." Are you looking forward to something but the waiting seems to be taking time. Maybe you're trusting God for the fruit of the womb, maybe for direction, maybe , a new job, a new car, a spouse, recovery from depression, sickness, debt?

The waiting room is never easy. I have been there many times. It is never easy. You feel the weight of the whole world on your shoulders and time seems to drag for eternity. Comforting words from those around you fall on dead ears because, to you, no one fully understands exactly how you feel. You search everywhere for the answers to the question "Why" but nothing seems to be enough. You look for someone to blame or even blame yourself. Yet, in reality, it's no one's fault.

What can you do while in the waiting room? Here are 7 of my best practices I have tried and tested myself:

1. **Pray:** Talking to God about it makes the load lighter. After all, He knows and sees each tear that falls.

2. **Praise:** Joy is a must. It can lift your spirit and prevent depression. When you find at least one thing to be thankful for every day, you develop an attitude of gratitude.

3. **Get busy:** While waiting, don't just do nothing. Find meaningful things to do to occupy your mind. Find your purpose in lief and pursue it- with or without the promise

4. **Help others:** A great way to get a blessing is by blessing others. Volunteer, help, encourage and mentor other people. it will all come back to you. As you see other people shine, let it encourage your heart that you are next in line.

5. **Stay hopeful:** Hope keeps dreams alive. Don't harbour bitterness.

6. **Keep the word close**: Keep God's word close to your heart. His promises come in handy when those limiting beliefs or doubt seem to cloud your view.

7. **Envision your future** and confess it daily. Call those things that be not as though they were and act as if you have it already.

Whatever it is you are going through today, I reach out to you in faith through this book. May you find grace to live, strength to conceive, patience to wait and unconditional joy in your heart. May God's favour shine on you and grant you victory. May He open doors for you that will cause you to smile again.

In your waiting, wait on God.

Let faith rise in your heart today.

He didn't bring you this far to leave you alone.

Hristiana Georgieva

Hristiana Georgieva is an empowerment and leadership consultant, with a background in IT, professional services and sales. She lives in London, UK and divides her time between IT sales and running her consulting business. Hristiana's passion has been writing ever since she was a little girl and being part of this project is a dream come true for her.

Web: *www.decisionvsdestiny.com*

Facebook: *www.facebook.com/decisionvsdestiny/*

IS THIS IT?

Is this it? The question has been at the back of my mind for a very long time but its constant chattering was now becoming undeniable. It was spring 2013. I was 31, married to a handsome man, I had been promoted a few months earlier and was doing well at my job. I was living the dream – solid above average income, had just finished decorating the beautiful home we'd bought together and my husband's business was thriving. As soon as I slowed down, however, and found a few quiet moments this nagging question would rush into my head in full force – Is this it?

I should have been incredibly happy, at the very least I should have been content! I had left home at 18, moved thousands of miles away from everything familiar to me so I could be and do anything I wanted. I was free wasn't I?

Growing up in a family of 5 I was the eldest of three sisters. It was in times when fortunes were changing daily in post Communist Bulgaria. I was sure that I was born in my small town full of narrow minded people with the singular purpose of leaving it all behind some day and doing something incredible. When the opportunity finally arrived, after a failed attempt or two, I was packing my bags to go study in the US! I was sure that this was it! This was where my incredible was going to happen.

Years of ups and downs followed. I met amazing people, continued to persevere through challenges and pushed on with the unyielding knowledge that things always get better, that as long as I could visualize my dreams they would come true. Wouldn't they?

Chasing this ultimate dream saw me leave NYC to move to Ireland in search of better opportunities. After many years of relentless pursuit of success I was about to make yet another move. It was 2010 I was happily engaged, established at work and moving to London!

Reflecting back to this move, I believe it was just as defining a move as leaving home at 18! I remember resisting the move immensely. My fiancée at the time just couldn't get a job offer despite many successful interviews and in the end I was the one who got a work transfer to the UK. Despite me getting the transfer I was very reluctant to rush the move. Dublin had become a home for me, I had friends and family there. I felt happy and free.

London meant facing my fiancée's family who were not very welcoming of me (different religion and culture), a city that I didn't really know and no friends. Being out-going and a resourceful individual I knew that the latter two were not an issue for me, at this point I had made two major life moves already and knew that it was much easier than people thought to set up a new life – the key was embracing it! Reflecting back on the events that would transpire over the next couple of years I wonder if intuitively I had an inkling I would be embarking on a true transformational journey that would change me.

When did I stop seeing the magic in the gentle twirls of the mist whilst driving on a tiny coast road in the West of Ireland? When did I become so obsessed with what I had and forgotten who I was? When did the deep feelings I thought I had for my husband disappear? The only thing left between us was the dubious bond over our only joint purpose left – to accumulate more?

My soul knew I had moved miles away from who I was, what I wanted and most importantly where I was going. It was longing to return to its natural state of innocent belief in possibility, in beauty, in grace and ease. Instead of listening to the warning signs in my mind, I deployed all of my resources into denying this knowledge. I convinced myself that happiness is a temporary sensation and the key to everything is been content. Why is it that we believe ourselves to be flying high when we are in fact falling? Here I was falling with the speed of light – I ate too much, instead of facing my truth. I worked too much, the only outlet for me to somewhat express myself and not have to face the fact that I was unhappy.

I didn't realize it at the time, but I ate to add a protective layer. I was hiding from the fact that I had given up who I truly was. I was relinquishing my power and living a life of pretend. I was pretending to be happy when in actuality I was miserable. Was the starry eyed girl full of hope and dreams dead? Had she forgotten all of her sometimes odd conversations with God? Was it this girl still full of dreams whispering the question, was this It? or was it God whispering to me in that ever present voice – whilst I continued to ignore the question is this it?

May 2013 I finally had enough. For the first time in a long time that tiny voice was heard loud and clear. I found myself in a car park by a MacDonald's knowing that I had to do something, that something had to change. As I sat there in my car, eating junk food and watching one of the most stunning sunsets over a nearly empty retail car park I was finally full of peace and knew with certainty that I would be OK.

It started with a flicker of hope at first ... It was that hope that reminded me of all I was capable of, it brought forward the certainty that no matter what happened I would be OK. I said a prayer, I do not remember the words although I think it must have been very personal and unorthodox, but I didn't care because my conversations with God had resumed!

Only 4 days later I found myself in a hospital ward wondering how I was going to come to terms with two stark facts:

- The doctor had just told me that my husband had a stroke and wouldn't live the night!

- I also found out that my husband had a mistress. She was actually the one to get him to the hospital. In fact she was there at his bedside!

You know the classic story that makes good soaps – well I sure did live through it that night at the end of May. The shock and the pain I had to go through in the hours and days that were to come at times felt unbearable.

God had answered my prayer for freedom, to be who he created me to be again. I had to dig my way through all the horrors that were between me and the hope I knew existed there someplace. I had to be stripped down to bare bones, face all the dark corners that I had ignored and let myself be ground down to dust so I could be forged again in a new image. I had to find the courage to look for hope, to look for light and find the belief that tomorrow would be better.

In the end it was that simple – three years later my life is very different. My now, ex-husband did survive his stroke although unfortunately partially disabled. I did however find a way to forgive him and move on – it came from the understanding that what he did, he did for himself and not to hurt me. My career began to soar, the right people started to come into my life, thankfully today I am surrounded by wonderful, loyal friends.

I've fallen in love again – with life and romantically. Importantly I have embraced that starry eyed girl and Follow my dreams of writing and teaching. As you read these very words know that they are a testimony that dreams do come true when you dare to hope, when you dare to dream.

I am so excited about the future. I know that regardless of how bad things get or how deeply you hurt that at the bottom of your personal box of life hope is always waiting to be unleashed in your heart. The only thing you need to do is dare to look for it.

Hope is the magical bridge that transports you from the dark night of your soul to the first rays of light on the other side of the horizon. Hope gives you the invisible wings that lift you up when you cannot find the strength to fight any longer. Hope is the beacon of light that calls the best of yourself forth and guides your ship to the safety of harbour and calm waters.What I learned and know for sure is that when you think there is nothing else left there is always hope.

Is hope another name of faith? Faith in tomorrow being a little bit better? Faith that you are strong enough, pretty enough, brave enough to get through whatever life may throw at you? Hope is the knowledge that even if it seems like there is no one there for you, you are never really alone.

I believe that faith is hope and hope is faith! It is that unyielding knowledge that whatever happens you will be OK, you will get through this, you will make it to another day. Hope is the singular driving force that elevates you to new levels.

Hope reminded me during one of my darkest hours of all that I was! It gave me the power to look up to the sky and make the bold statement that I refused to be defeated by my circumstances. It was the quintessential ingredient that facilitated the transformation I went through.

So how does one find hope? To me it started with a simple prayer, a statement that I will not succumb into the darkness that was taking over my life. I asked and I was given – the support, the opportunities, the wonderful friends, this life that gets better and better. Hope, the remembrance of grace, of the presence of God, of that benevolent force that will always guide you home.

Should you find yourself lost in the darkest of all your nights then I ask you this – go light a candle and as its golden light breaks through the dusk, ask for hope to enter your life more abundantly. Remember that there were others before you who found themselves at the edge of the world, staring at a dark abyss and yet they found the strength to go forth. Use this knowledge to prop yourself up and let this carry you forward. My gift to you is this. Until your own hope whispers in your ear, gives you the strength to go on, not just to endure but to truly thrive, grab a ray of hope from my story, hold onto it and find hope knowing that you to can overcome anything in your life that tries to steal your hope, your sparkle for life. Just know that whatever it is you are facing you are never alone.

Chapter 6

LOOKING FORWARD WITH RENEWED HOPE

Job 11:17-18

"Then your life shall be brighter than the noonday; its gloom shall become as the morning, and you shall be secure, because there is hoped you shall look around you and lie down in safety."

I hope you are able to find encouragement in the stories that were shared with you in Chapter 5. Take a moment to really know, to let is sink into your heart, that just as these people overcame you too can overcome.

No matter if you are struggling with fertility issues or going through the loss of someone special in your life, gain strength in knowing you don't travel the journey of life alone. Reach out, allow others to be there as a support system to you, connect with others who have or are going through the same struggles and overcoming them. Change can be difficult but staying the same in the long term will bring much more pain. Hope comes in the process of change and growth!

On the next pages you will find the 10 Keys to Hold Onto Hope Even When it all Seems Hopeless. Use these keys as blocks in which to build your hope back up.

10 KEYS TO HOLD ONTO HOPE EVEN WHEN IT ALL SEEMS HOPELESS

1. **Gratitude:** Develop an attitude of gratitude, even in the small things, daily develop your attitude of gratitude, in all things be grateful.

2. **Journaling:** write your way through pain to a life of joy: using a journal to express your thoughts, feelings, and experiences will enable you to get it out instead of keeping it inside and allowing it to occupy the space in your brain that becomes relentless.

3. **Community**: Reach out those in your community who can be sources of hope for you. Community is one way in which you can ensure you don't place yourself into isolation.

4. **Help Others**: Often, through helping others your own hope can be renewed. Joy can be found in helping others in their journeys to overcome as well. Be open to extending your hand of help to those who need it.

5. **Reading**: Try and read from the bible every day. It can be such a great source of hope. You can also read books that encourage you and inspire you.

6. **Embracing your Talents and Gifts**: Find classes in your local area that you would enjoy and take part. Try something new that you have always wanted to do. Really embrace the talents and gifts that God has given to

you and try and incorporate them every day.

7. **Relaxation**: Take time out of those busy days to relax with those you love, or with your favourite up of tea. Really make time to decompress and just "BE" rather than doing all the time.

8. **Self-care**: Make sure you take time to take care for yourself as well. This can be as easy as taking 5 min a night before bed to stretch.

9. **Reaching Out**: Don't be afraid to reach out to others when you need help or if you need a shoulder to cry on. Know who those trusted people are and go to them when you need them. People can't read your mind and may not know you need something if you don't express it.

10. **Prayer and Reflection**: Make prayer a regular priority and take time to reflect. This can bring you to new awakenings which God will reveal to you in order that your life may become better. Ask others to pray for you.

If you know someone is really struggling in their lives reach out and give them a hug, be a support to them, or help them find others who will be able to provide the kind of support they need.

Much blessings and hope on your journey,

Kristy-Lea Tritz

"Everything in life is a journey. It isn't about perfection on that journey. It is about growth and deeper intimacy with God. The more you embrace the journey and allow your past pains and challenges to turn into blessings, the more your life will be blessed!"

~Kristy-Lea Tritz